VI COMMANDS

Command	Description
vi *filename*	Opens *filename* at beginning.
a	Appends text one character to right of cursor.
A	Appends text at end of line.
b	Moves cursor back one word.
cc	Lets you change a line and continue in insert mode.
Ctrl-B	Scrolls back a full screen.
Ctrl-D	Scrolls down half a screenful.
Ctrl-E	Scrolls screen up a line.
Ctrl-F	Scrolls forward a full screen.
Ctrl-R	Refreshes the screen (clears stray characters).
cw	Lets you change a word and continue in insert mode.
dd	Deletes a whole line.
D	Deletes the rest of current line.
dw	Deletes a word.
h	Moves cursor to the left one space.
H	Moves cursor to top of screen (High).
i	Inserts text at cursor position.
I	Inserts text at beginning of line.
k	Moves cursor up one line.
l	Moves cursor one space to the right.
L	Moves cursor to bottom of screen (Low).
M	Moves cursor to middle of screen (Middle).
nG	Moves cursor to line number n.
:n	Moves cursor to line number n.
o	Opens a line to insert text below the cursor.
O	Opens a line to insert text above the cursor.
:q!	Quits vi and cancel all changes to file.
r	Lets you replace a character and return to escape mode.
/text	Searches forward through file for text.
?text	Searches backward through file for text.
u	Undoes last text-altering command.
w	Moves cursor forward one word.
:w	Saves your last changes; writes file to hard disk.

The ABC's of
SCO UNIX

The ABC's of
SCO UNIX

Tom Cuthbertson

SYBEX ®

San Francisco • Paris • Düsseldorf • Soest

Acquisitions Editor: Dianne King
Editor: Winifred Kelly
Technical Editor: Arthur Evans
Word Processors: Lisa Mitchell, Ann Dunn, and Scott Campbell
Series Designer: Suzanne Albertson
Chapter Art and Layout: Ingrid Owen
Typesetter: Stephanie Hollier
Proofreaders/Production Assistants: Rhonda M. Holmes and Dina Quan
Indexer: Ted Laux
Cover Designer: Thomas Ingalls + Associates
Cover Photographer: Mark Johann

Library of Congress Card Number: 90-71523

ISBN: 0-89588-715-0

Manufactured in the United States of America

10 9 8 7 6 5 4 3 2 1

For Colleen

ACKNOWLEDGMENTS

Many thanks to Arthur Evans and Winnie Kelly, my patient and thorough editors.

Thanks also to these among the many others who helped me so generously with this book:

Dianne King, Lori Heit Lyons, Jeff Hill, Jim Jones, Matt Brocchini, Dan Jungwirth, Stewart Chapman, Allan Heim, Wing Eng, Andrew Muir, Kirk Strong, Stewart Evans, Bob Stayton, Hanna Nelson, Doug Robert, Eric Williams, David Bedno, David Vangerov, Lisa and Brian Pufahl Cox, Bart Abicht, Nina Paley, and my co-workers at SCO.

CONTENTS AT A GLANCE

TABLE OF CONTENTS

T H R E E

Using
Electronic Mail

F O U R

Learning about
Files and
Directories

F I V E

Saving Copies
of Your Files

S I X

Printing
with UNIX

N I N E

Advanced vi
Techniques

INTRODUCTION

Welcome to UNIX. UNIX is the operating system that makes the most efficient use of the power available in modern personal computers. With UNIX, a computer that was made for one user can meet all the computing needs of a dozen users or more. *That's efficiency.* If you are working on a UNIX computer system, you, and everyone else on the system, can do several tasks at once. *That's power.*

This book tells you how to take advantage of all that computing power, no matter how much or how little computer experience you have. If you have never used a computer, follow each step very carefully and read all the explanatory material that accompanies each procedure. If you have some computer experience, but are new to UNIX systems, you can go through the procedures more quickly, using the first sentence of each step to guide you, and skimming the text to find the explanations of UNIX concepts that are new to you.

If you have a problem with a procedure in any of the following chapters, look for a Troubleshooting section at the end of the chapter, to see if a solution to your problem is listed. If you can't find a solution to the problem there, check the index to see if the problem is covered in another chapter.

First, we'll introduce you to the basic skills you need to begin using your UNIX system. Chapter 1 describes the components of your UNIX system and tells you how to log in and log out. Chapter 2 shows you how to write and edit a short file, and how you can use it on the UNIX system. In Chapter 3, you learn about electronic mail: how to write electronic mail messages, how to read through messages you have received, and how to deal with these messages.

Then we cover the skills you need to keep your work in order on your UNIX system. Chapter 4 describes the UNIX file system and tells you how to organize your files so you can find them and use them conveniently. Chapter 5 teaches you how to save files from your computer's hard disk to a floppy disk or a tape archive. Chapter 6 shows you how to produce printed versions of files on your UNIX system.

Last, you learn about additional programs and skills you can use to enhance your productivity on the UNIX system. Chapter 7 introduces SCO's menu and window interface, Office Portfolio. Chapter 8 describes three applications you can use on your UNIX system: Microsoft Word, a word-processing program; SCO Professional, a spreadsheet program; and FoxBASE +, a database program. Chapter 9 teaches advanced vi skills, increasing your abilities with the screen text editor. Chapter 10 tells how to customize your work environment on the UNIX system, and how to solve some serious terminal and system problems that may occur.

The most important thing you can learn about UNIX is that all of its power and efficiency are readily available to you once you grasp the basic ideas of how to use it. Yes, UNIX is complex. It offers a great number of features to a great number of different types of users, so it can seem quite formidable to you when you face it for the first time. But with the help of this book, you can learn how to handle all of the basic UNIX functions, and go on to do whatever *you* need to do for your job. The beauty of UNIX is that once you learn the basics, you can branch out and do whatever you want to do; there is always more computing power available to you. With the help of this book, you can take advantage of it.

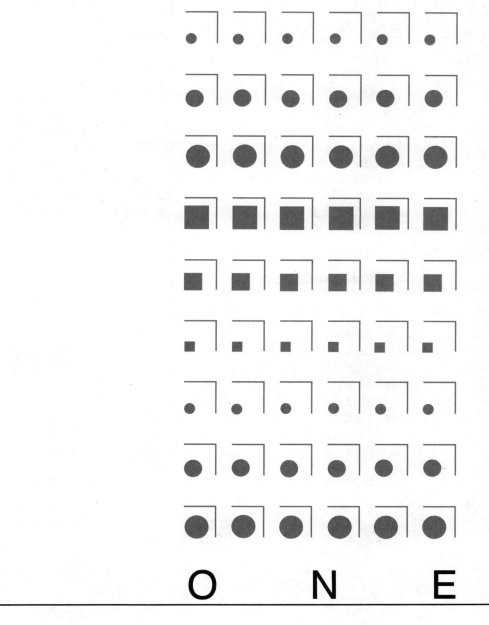

O N E

Getting
Started

This chapter tells you how to get ready to work on your UNIX system. We'll take a look at the system first, then show you how to log in to the system at the terminal where you're going to work. This chapter also tells you how to log out, so you can stop working on the UNIX system whenever you want.

If you're completely new to computers, you may wonder what it means to "log in" and "log out", or even just what a UNIX system is. Fear not. You will learn these things one at a time. Let's start with what a UNIX system is.

UNIX System Basics

A UNIX system is simply a computer and other pieces of computer equipment connected together. Your UNIX system probably consists of a computer, at least one printer, and several terminals. These pieces of equipment are known as the hardware. A simple UNIX system is shown in Figure 1.1.

Your terminal is the piece of hardware you work with most. It consists of the keyboard you type on and the TV-like monitor you look at. When you type at the keyboard, you see the words and numbers on the monitor screen. You type commands to tell the computer

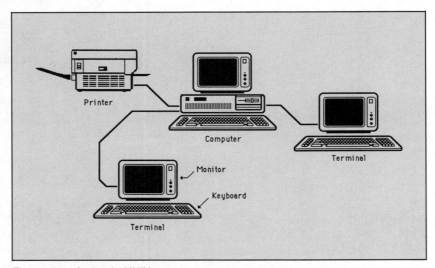

Figure 1.1: A simple UNIX system

what to do for you. The computer reports things back to you or prints them out on the printer.

There are coded instructions in the computer that accept your commands and carry out the work you ask for. These instructions are the *software,* programs that engineers have written to do various tasks. On any computer system, it is the software that makes the hardware work for you.

The thing that makes a UNIX system different from other computer systems is the UNIX software, the coded set of instructions that allows the pieces of hardware to work together very efficiently, and very fast.

The key piece of UNIX software is the *operating system.* An operating system controls the interactions of your commands, other users' commands, and other software, which the commands call on to do things like write text, plan a budget, or record complex data.

UNIX's operating system, unlike many other operating systems, can handle more than one command at once. For example, if you want to find some obscure and complex set of facts in a database, you can send a command to the computer to look it up for you. While it is doing the search, you can write a message to a fellow worker and send it over electronic mail. The UNIX operating system can do more than one task for you at a time; this is why it is called a *multitasking* operating system.

In the same way, the UNIX operating system handles multiple overlapping commands, allowing other users on the system to send commands to the same computer to look for things in the database and send mail messages, too. For this reason, it is also called a *multiuser* operating system; it lets multiple users give multiple commands to the same computer at the same time. Obviously, there is a clear business advantage to a multiuser operating system. A company can buy one computer that ten people can use at the same time, rather than having to buy ten computers for ten people.

How does the UNIX operating system handle all those commands at once? The answer to this question is quite complex, but the key idea is the division of work between a *kernel* and numerous *shells.* The kernel is the processing center of the operating system; shells are individual sessions or processes of the UNIX program. There are different types of shells: your system may use the Bourne shell, or the C-shell, for instance. Each time you start to use UNIX, you create a new shell of whatever type your system uses. Starting a new process sometimes also starts a new shell. Each new shell is a new session of UNIX, with the same power as any other shell. Shells geometrically increase UNIX's ability to process individual commands.

When you give a command to the computer, a shell interprets the command so that the kernel can process it, and arranges to share the computer's processing time efficiently with other shells. When the kernel completes a task, the results of the kernel's work are returned to you by way of the shell again, which presents them to you in a usable form. Figure 1.2 shows a schematic drawing of a kernel and some shells.

The shells and the kernel work together somewhat like the waiters and kitchen staff do at a restaurant. You, the computer user, are like the customer. You give a command to your shell, the way a customer gives an order to a waiter. The waiter takes the order into the kitchen, where all kinds of things happen (arcane and tedious things best left unseen). After a while, the waiter brings your meal back out to you. In a similar way, your command is carried by the shell into the UNIX kernel, to a program that "cooks" it. Then the shell brings the output back to your terminal screen for you to view. You can have more than one shell working for you at a time, too, just as one waiter may be taking away your dirty dishes while another is bringing you your coffee. Figure 1.3 shows the UNIX cafe in action.

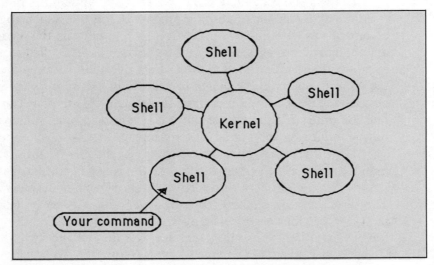

Figure 1.2: The UNIX operating system's kernel and shells

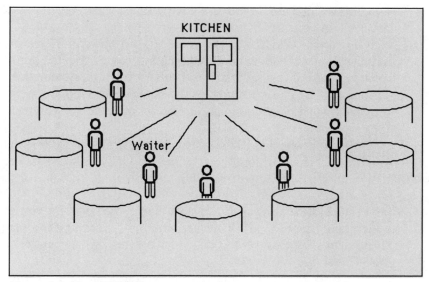

Figure 1.3: *The UNIX Cafe*

Things happen much faster on a UNIX system than in a restaurant. The shell, the kernel, and the programs work at near the speed of light, for one thing. But in the same way that the one big stove in a restaurant kitchen can be cooking twenty different customers' food at the same time, the main transistor chip in your system's central computer can be processing twenty commands at once; the UNIX kernel cook just has to do a lot of jumping back and forth, keeping all those processes going, and sending them back out to the users' shells when they are done.

This book will teach you how to communicate effectively with the computer, sending it the commands that will put both the hardware and the software to work for you, and making your job easier. But before you can start sending commands and getting results from the computer, you have to log in to the UNIX system.

Before You Log In

Logging in is the process of telling the system who you are. To log in, you need to know your *login name:* the name you have been assigned within UNIX. You also have to know what type of passwords are used on your UNIX system.

For most UNIX systems, there is a system administrator who handles things like login names and passwords. A system administrator takes care of the hardware and software on the system and helps people who use it. Depending on the size of your UNIX system, you may have a full-time system administrator or someone who has other jobs as well.

Find out who acts as the system administrator on your system. If you are new to using computers or new to UNIX, make sure the system administrator knows this. Make sure that it is all right for you to ask for help.

The system administrator has made an *account* for you on the system and named it with your login name. An account is a place on the system where you will keep your work; every user on the system has at least one.

Ask your system administrator for your login name. (Some system administrators call it a *username* rather than a login name.) It will probably be an abbreviation of your full name: mine is *tomc,* for instance. Whatever yours is, memorize it. Notice that your login name has no uppercase letters and no spaces in it. You have to spell it with lowercase letters and no spaces, or UNIX won't recognize you when you try to log in. UNIX is particular about uppercase and lowercase letters, unlike DOS and some other operating systems.

After your system administrator has told you your login name, ask what sort of password security measures there are on your UNIX system. Passwords can provide excellent security for everyday office needs, if you use them properly. They are used on most systems to keep outsiders from logging in and poking around in your private work.

Your administrator usually gives you a temporary or "default" password, just so you can log in the first time. Then you make up your own password, so nobody knows it but you. If the administrator gives you a temporary password, memorize it carefully. After the system administrator tells it to you, repeat it slowly and clearly for the administrator to hear; make sure you say which letters, if any, are uppercase. Remember, UNIX is particular about uppercase and lowercase letters, and passwords, unlike login names, often have some uppercase letters in them.

On a very few systems, you may not need a password at all; you can skip all the material on passwords in this chapter.

OK. You know your login name or user name, and if you were given a password, you memorized it. You're ready to log in. One note before you start: if you have problems, look at the Troubleshooting section at the end of the chapter. If that doesn't help, see your system administrator.

*L*ogging In

1. Turn your terminal on, if it isn't on already.

Press the spacebar on the keyboard. If nothing appears on the monitor screen, turn the contrast knob and see if anything changes. If not, the terminal is probably off. The on/off switch is usually on one side of the monitor or on the back, but it may not be easy to find. Manufacturers hide the power switches in places where they will not be bumped by accident. If your terminal's switch is hard to find, ask your system administrator where it is. Don't be embarrassed to ask this question; anybody can have trouble finding the power switch on a terminal they've never seen before. Figure 1.4 shows a typical UNIX terminal.

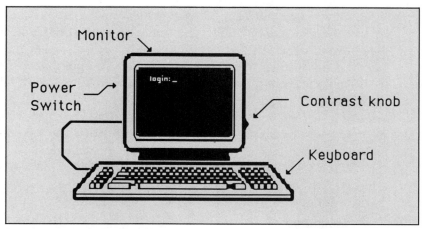

Figure 1.4: *A typical UNIX terminal*

When you turn your terminal on, some self-testing messages may appear, and there may be a beep or two. When things calm down, you should see a login prompt and a cursor.

login:_

The login prompt (the word *login* and its colon) is asking you to log in. The *cursor* is either a box or a short underline showing you where you are on the screen. It may blink, or it may not, depending on how things are set up on your terminal. If all you see is a cursor, press the Return key a few times. The login prompt should appear. If it doesn't, see the Troubleshooting section at the end of this chapter.

2. Enter your login name.

Type it in just as the system administrator told you, and remember not to use any uppercase letters. If you make a mistake typing, use the Backspace key to back over the mistake, then type in your login name correctly. When you get it right, press the Return key. Although no symbol for the Return key appears on the screen, pressing the Return key is essential. It signals the end of a command or response, so that UNIX will process it and reply to you. Whenever you type a command, always end it with a Return.

If you are using a keyboard that is new to you, become familiar with the positions of the Return, Control, Escape, Backspace, and Delete keys. The Return key may say "Enter" on it, or may be marked by a bent arrow pointing down and to the left (←┘). The Control key may have the letters "Ctrl" or "CTL" on it. The Escape key may say "Esc" on it. The Backspace key may have an arrow pointing to the left (←). The Delete key may say "Del" or DEL on it. See Figure 1.5 for the locations of these five special keys on three common styles of keyboard. If your keyboard doesn't seem to have one of the above keys, see your system administrator; on some keyboards, you have to use alternate keys to do the things the special keys usually do.

When you have pressed the Return key, a password prompt appears. Now that UNIX knows who you are, it asks you for your password. For example, when I log in, my screen looks like this:

login: tomc
Password: _

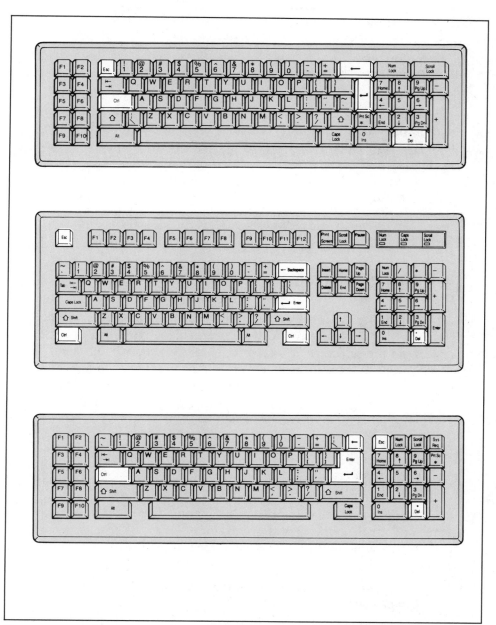

Figure 1.5: The location of the special keys on some common keyboards

If you see something similar to this, go on to step 3, below. If I didn't need a password, I would see this:

login: tomc
Password:
$ _

The dollar sign is my system prompt. Yours might not be a dollar sign; it might be a **%** sign, or something else entirely. You might also see a **TERM =** prompt. If you see any of these prompts, skip step 3 and go on to step 4.

If you see no prompt at all, press the Return key once or twice. Still no prompt? See the Troubleshooting section at the end of this chapter.

3. Enter the temporary password your system administrator gave you.

Type it in exactly as you were told. When you have typed in the password, press the Return key. Notice that the password doesn't appear on the screen as you type it. That's to keep wily hackers—people trying to log in illegally—from looking over your shoulder and copying your password. Although this is a good security measure, typing something you can't see is a bit tricky. Don't worry about making a mistake, though; if you do, you'll see this:

login:tomc
Password:
Login incorrect
login: _

You get another chance, free of charge. Just enter your user name and the temporary password again.

If you enter your login name and the password correctly, something like this should appear:

Your password has expired. Choose a new one.
Old password:

Enter the temporary password again. If you do it correctly, you'll see the following message:

Enter new password (minimum of 5 characters)
Please use a combination of upper and lowercase letters and numbers.
New password:

Now it's time to make up your own password. (If you see only a system prompt instead of the request above, you have to do a little more work to create your new password; see chapter 10.)

Keep the following guidelines in mind as you make up a password. It should be five to eight letters or numbers long, and at least one letter should be uppercase. It can be longer, but don't create one that is so long you can't memorize it. Your password should be easy for you to remember and type, but tough for anybody else to guess. Common names of relatives, pets, and cars are not good passwords; they can be guessed at too easily by hackers. It's a good idea to use more than one word, separated by meaningless characters instead of spaces. Single words that might be found in an on-line dictionary, especially the UNIX dictionary, are useless as passwords. A hacker can try all of the words in the dictionary as passwords with a simple program.

An unusual password that means something to you but nothing to other people is ideal. For me, *lockMup* is a good one. It's the name of my favorite local mountain bike trail; I'll never forget it, but it means nothing to other people. Of course, now that I've told you, I can never use it; a password loses its value the moment you tell it to anybody.

When you have thought up a unique, personal password, enter it and press the Return key. If the password is too short or it doesn't have both lowercase and uppercase characters, a message appears, telling you to try again. When you enter an acceptable password, a message asks you to re-enter it:

New password:
Re-enter new password:

UNIX wants you to be sure you entered the password you want, since it's easy to make a mistake when you can't see what you entered.

Enter the password again. If you made a mistake either time, you'll see the message:

They don't match: try again

Start the process of making your own password over again. If you made up one that was too hard to type, try one that's still unique, but easier to type. When you enter your password the same way twice, your screen clears. Then you may see a message or two. Some systems require you to log in again, as a double security precaution.

4. Enter your terminal type.

When the password messages are done, and you have logged in again (if you were prompted to), you may see something like this:

TERM = (unknown)

The word TERM is short for Terminal. Unknown means UNIX doesn't know what kind of terminal you have. UNIX can work with most terminal types, but it needs to know what it's dealing with, so that it knows which keys are available on your keyboard, and how to communicate properly with your screen. If you don't know what type of terminal you're sitting in front of, or if you don't know the correct abbreviation, ask your system administrator. Enter the correct abbreviation and press the Return key.

On some systems, UNIX may already know your terminal type. For example, if you have a Wyse 60 terminal, some systems say "TERM = (wy60)". If that's the case, just hit the Return key to confirm the TERM statement.

When you press the Return key after specifying your terminal type, you will probably see a message confirming it, and then you should see the system prompt. On some systems, there may be other questions or messages; see your administrator if you can't figure out what they mean. In the end, if you have logged in successfully, you see the system prompt:

$ _

Congrats! You're in. You can now start exploring the world of UNIX.

About Your System Prompt

You can write commands for your UNIX system whenever your cursor appears next to the system prompt. On most UNIX systems, **$** is used as the system prompt. On some systems, the **%** prompt is used. There may even be some other prompt on your system.

The kind of prompt you have indicates what type of shell you're using. If you have a **$** prompt, you are using the Bourne (pronounced *born*) shell. We will use the Bourne shell in all examples in this book. If you have a **%** prompt, you are using the C-shell. Most of the basic commands explained in this book have the same effect in both the C-shell and the Bourne shell. In those cases where C-shell commands differ from Bourne-shell commands, it will be noted in the instructions.

If you have neither a **$** nor a **%** prompt, and your prompt makes no sense to you, ask your system administrator what shell you are using.

Entering Commands

Now let's try some commands out, and see what they do.

1. Enter the who command.

Enter the command all by itself, as shown:

$ who

When you press the Return key, you see something like this:

```
$ who
galeg      tty07    Oct 09 08:04:15
tracyf     tty04    Oct 09 08:01:15
tomc       tty02    Oct 09 10:03:00
georgei    tty03    Oct 09 07:11:30
mattc      tty05    Oct 09 10:12:00
```

The who command tells you who is logged in on the system, which terminal connections they are using, and when they logged in. It looks like georgei was the early bird; tomc and mattc were a little slow getting started this morning.

2. Use the who command with arguments.

Enter the following three words, as shown:

$ who am i

Make sure you enter the command just like it looks, small **i** and all. When you hit the Return key, you'll see something like this:

$ who am i
tomc tty02 Oct 9 10:03:00

UNIX tells you your login name, the terminal connection you're using, and the date and time when you last logged in. In this case, it's telling me that I am logged in as tomc, using terminal 2, and that I logged in on October 9 at three minutes past ten.

The words **am i** make the command **who** more specific. They are called the command's *arguments*. They add to the basic command's meaning.

3. Use the who command with an option.

If there aren't many people logged in, you might not have seen much of a display when you entered the **who** command. But try entering it with a **-l** (a hyphen and an "el") after it:

$ who -l

Whoosh! A lot of information probably appeared on your screen, and some of it may have whizzed right off the top as more and more appeared on the bottom. Most of the lines of data probably look something like this:

LOGIN	**tty005**	**Sep 30**	**14:05**	**old**	**153**
LOGIN	**ttyp29**	**Sep 30**	**14:12**	**old**	**3512**
LOGIN	**ttyT 5**	**Oct 08**	**17:19**	**6:08**	**2495**

Why all those LOGINS?. The **-l** you put after **who** is an *option,* or *flag.* Like an argument, an option changes or refines a command's meaning. An option is always a hyphen with a single letter, which is usually *mnemonic*—it helps you remember what the option does.

The -l option used with the **who** command displays a list of terminals that are free for people to *l*og into (hence the *l*). The date and time the terminal was last logged into are shown, and how long ago the terminal last received a command (*old* means more than 24 hours ago). The last number identifies the last process that ran on the terminal.

4. Enter the date command.

Now let's try another common, useful command: **date**. To do this, simply enter:

$ date

The **date** command tells UNIX to display the current time and date on your screen. When you hit the Return key, the following message appears:

$ date
Mon Oct 9 10:45:30 PST 1991

The computer reads a digital clock that runs inside it, and tells you the day, month, date, time (in hours, minutes, and seconds), the time zone it's using, and the current year.

5. Edit mistakes in a command.

Now that you know some commands, it's time to make some mistakes and see how to correct them. For instance, try entering:

$ fate

This is a mistake anybody could make; hitting the **f** instead of the **d** while trying to enter the **date** command. UNIX just responds by saying:

$ fate
fate:not found
$.

Note that after UNIX says it couldn't find that command, it gives you your system prompt again. So even though UNIX won't let you command the fates, it doesn't penalize you for goofing. Try entering **DATE** or **Date** or even **datE**. UNIX can't find any of those commands; it is very particular about uppercase and lowercase, as you can see.But if you enter **date** again, bingo, you're rewarded with the time and date. How about adding an option? It worked with **who**— let's try **date -l**.

On my system, I get the following response:

```
$ date -l
date: no TOY clock
Usage: date [MMddhhmm[yy]] [ + format]
$
```

The gist of the first message line is, "don't play with date". A system administrator can use the **date** command to set the date for your whole UNIX system. Since UNIX knows from your login name that you aren't a system administrator, it doesn't want you to do anything other than get a quick look at today's date.

The **Usage:** message line tells you ways you can change or refine how the **date** command is carried out. As you can see, UNIX does let you change the look or the format of the date.

6. Enter a customized command.

Many commands can be customized with options and arguments that give very specific instructions to UNIX. For instance, try this:

```
$ date ' + %a, %h %d, 19%y; my first day in UNIX'
```

You may have to try a few times to get this right: make sure you get the spaces and single quotes in the right places. When you get everything right, hit the Return key; you'll see the following nifty message:

```
Fri, Oct 09, 1991; my first day in UNIX
```

The quotes with a plus sign tell UNIX that you want the date result back in that specific format. The **%a, %h, %d,** and **%y** are *variables,* which UNIX replaces with the proper information from its clock: the day for **%a**, the month for **%h**, and so on. The other information is sent back to you just as you typed it in.

Your date will be different, of course, but it is a big day for you; it's your first day on a UNIX system, and you're already writing customized commands!

Logging Out

Whenever you stop working on the UNIX system, you'll need to log yourself out. The procedure is very simple.

1. Make sure the cursor is at the system prompt.

Press the Return key if you are on a line with an unfinished command. Even if you are already at the system prompt, it doesn't hurt to hit the Return key a time or two. It just does this:

```
$da
da:not found
$
$
$ _
```

2. At the system prompt, enter exit.

That's all there is to it. On some systems, you can use Ctrl-d (hold down the Control key and press **d**) instead of entering **exit**. If you are the C shell (your proumpt is a **%**) type **logout** and press Return. When you have successfully logged out, the system prompt is replaced by the login prompt, like this:

```
$ exit
login:
```

Now the terminal is ready to be used by someone else.

You should log out every time you leave your terminal for any length of time. If you aren't using the system, the polite thing to do is to get off it so other users can have more access to it. It's like freeing up your table at the restaurant, so that somebody else can sit down and start ordering things from the waiter.

There is another very good reason to log out. If you leave your terminal without logging out, somebody can come along and use your terminal and your account, and therefore the whole UNIX system, in your name. A hacker might weasel his way into files on the system posing as you. Even worse, someone who doesn't have much else to do can come around, check your terminal, find that you are logged in, and then send embarrassing messages to all of the other users on the system, like *I think the boss is a space case,* or *I'm such a space case I left myself logged in tonight.* If it happens to you once, you never forget the lesson again: log out before you leave.

Troubleshooting

I don't see the login prompt.

Make sure your terminal is turned on; the switch is usually on one of the sides of the monitor or on the back of it. Check the brightness control, too; it's usually at the front of the monitor. Terminal bright and ready? Press the Return key a few times. No luck? Hold down the Control key and press **Q** several times. If you can find a Break key on your keyboard, press it and the Return key alternately. If all you see is a cursor, you may have a modem, rather than a hardwire connection between your terminal and the computer. To learn how to dial in on a modem, see "Using UNIX Over a Modem" in Chapter 10.

If you don't have a modem and all you see is a cursor, the data line to your terminal may be unplugged or loose. You should have two cords connected to the back of your terminal; the power cord and the data line. Plug them both in firmly and press the Return key again. If you still don't see anything other than the cursor, or if you see nothing at all, see your system administrator. Either the UNIX system is down, or your terminal is broken.

Nothing happens after I log in.

You did press the Return key, didn't you? Wait for a minute after you press it. The system may be slow at the moment—even the best UNIX systems can have slow moments. If nothing happens for several moments, ask other users if they are having problems. If so, see your system administrator.

I get a message about lowercase letters when I enter my login name.

You entered some uppercase letters when typing in your login name. The message will read something like this:

If your terminal supports lowercase letters, please use them. Login again, using lowercase if possible.

Do as the message suggests. Make sure you enter your name in all lowercase letters (like **bethj** rather than **BethJ** or **Bethj**). On some systems, instead of giving you a polite message, the terminal just displays every character you type, regardless of case, as an uppercase character.

Everything is in uppercase letters.

If the word LOGIN is in uppercase, and everything you type comes out in upper-case letters, the UNIX system has the mistaken idea that your terminal can only display uppercase characters. Any terminal that is made for UNIX use can handle both uppercase and lowercase characters. If you start the login process over, your terminal should be able to use both lowercase and uppercase letters. Press the Delete key or enter **Ctrl-d** to start the login process over. When you finish logging in, letters should appear in the correct case. If not, see your system administrator.

I typed my login name wrong.

If you make a typing mistake while entering your login name, just press the Return key. When the password prompt appears, press the Return key again. You will see the **Login incorrect** message, and then the login prompt, telling you to try again.

My backspace key doesn't work.

Try holding the Control key down and pressing **h**. If this doesn't work either, try the # key (Shift-3). Still no luck? You have an odd terminal, or one that needs special attention. See your system administrator.

I see the message
Disconnected *and the login prompt returns.*

You waited too long to type your password. Enter your login name again, and when you see the password prompt, type your password, carefully but promptly.

I see the message tput: unknown
Terminal_____ *or* Terminal type unknown.

If you see the first message, the terminal type you entered appears in the blank. Either message indicates you entered a terminal type that UNIX does not recognize. Log out and log in again. This time, make sure you enter your terminal type correctly; check with your system administrator to get the spelling right. If you still get an error message, the terminal may be set up incorrectly; have your system administrator set it up again.

Gibberish appears on my screen.

If you have logged in over a modem, you probably are having transmission problems, or your modem is acting up. See "Using UNIX Over a Modem" in Chapter 10. If you are not using a modem, either you are getting garbled messages from the system, or your terminal is acting up. In either case, see your system administrator.

*C*ommand Summary

COMMAND	DESCRIPTION
loginname	Enter your own login name at the **login:** prompt to access your account on UNIX.
password	Enter your own password at the **password:** prompt to confirm your identity.
who	Shows who is currently using the system.
who am i	Shows your account name, your terminal number, and when you logged in

COMMAND	DESCRIPTION
who -l	Shows terminals currently free to be used.
date	Shows the UNIX system date.
exit	Exits your account on UNIX. On some systems, you can use **Ctrl-d** as well.

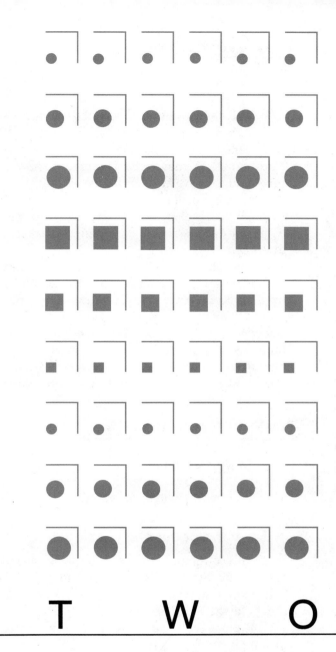

T W O

Writing and Editing Text with vi

This chapter introduces you to writing on the UNIX system. You learn by writing and editing a file, using the UNIX screen-editing program called vi. It's pronounced *vee-eye* (for *vi*sual). It was the first text editor on UNIX that enabled users to see a whole screenful of text at a time, and to move around the file visually. Previous UNIX editors let you see only one line of text at a time.

This chapter explains how to use vi to enter text, and how to edit what you have written, correcting mistakes, adding new text, and deleting unwanted text.

The file you will create as you work through this chapter is a reminder file. It will contain a list of dates and a reminder of what you need to do on each date. It will give you plenty of practice word-processing with vi, with an added bonus: UNIX has a program called calendar, which can take your reminder file and use it to send you reminder messages every day. At the end of the chapter, you'll learn how to put this file to work for you. UNIX will then automatically show you each reminder on the day when you need it.

Beginning a vi Session

To write a reminder file, you need to open vi and then enter the text. You have to be logged in, with the cursor at the system prompt. Then use the following procedure.

1. Enter the command vi calendar *at the system prompt.*

This command opens a vi file called calendar. If you make a typing mistake, just backspace over it and type in the command correctly. When you press the Return key, the screen clears, then you see something like the screen shown in Figure 2.1.

Right away, you know you're in new territory: your system prompt is gone, for one thing. There's a column of tildes (˜) down the left side of the screen, and a message at the bottom of the screen, telling you that you've started a new file called "calendar". The tildes are line markers, showing you the empty lines after the end of your text. Since you haven't written any text yet, the whole screen is filled with empty lines. Your system prompt is gone because you are now inside the vi world. You can't give commands the way you do at the system prompt.

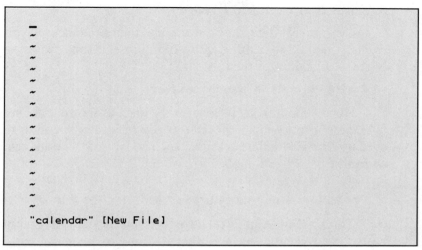

Figure 2.1: *A newly-opened vi file*

2. Enter the i command to go into insert mode.

Enter **i** so you are ready to type in *i*nsert mode. Try typing **vi** again. The letters appear, but it doesn't work as a command now—it's just text. If you hit the Return key, you don't get a "New file" message. You just see the cursor go down to the next line, like this:

vi

‾
~

~

Why? Because you are now "inside" vi, in insert mode, so the computer sees everything you insert as text, not commands. If you want to enter a command in vi, you have to get into *escape* mode. You will learn various ways to do this in a minute.

Entering Text in vi

Once you have gone into insert mode, you can begin to type text in vi, just as if you were using a typewriter. The following procedure explains this in detail.

1. Enter text from the keyboard.

Type today's date, then a space, and then a reminder to yourself, telling you to do something today. In my case, if today were the 14th of April, I might type the following:

4/14 Put water in the car radiator_

Use the month/day format for the date, as shown. And keep the reminder short (less than one line). If you make a typing mistake, just back up over it with the Backspace key, and type the date and reminder correctly.

2. Press the Return key and enter another line of text.

Think of something you have to do on a specific day within the next week. Write the date and what you have to do on the new line of your calendar file. Next Thursday I have to pay the piano teacher, for instance, so my file now looks like this:

vi
4/14 Put water in the car radiator
4/18 Pay Louise for piano lesson_

Be careful not to use an **O** (uppercase o) instead of a **0** (zero), or an **l** (lowercase L) instead of a **1** (one). UNIX doesn't recognize those substitutions, and the file you are writing is going to be read by UNIX; you want to be sure it can send you the correct reminder on the correct date.

3. Type a line with a mistake in it.

Type an extra space in the date. UNIX is particular about things like spaces; a line with one extra space in the date will confuse UNIX when it reads your calendar file:

4/ 19 Scottish dance class_

UNIX wouldn't be able to read this date when the day came, and I might forget to go kick up my heels. In order to get rid of that extra space, I could backspace all the way back to it and type the whole line over. But vi has a better, quicker way.

*E*diting Text in vi

Up until now, we've been working in insert mode. To edit text, you need use a second mode—escape mode. In escape mode you can give commands and move around the file to edit different parts of the text you have entered.

1. Enter escape mode to edit previously inserted text.

Press the Escape key. You are now out of insert mode. Once you're in escape mode (or command mode, as some people say) you can move all around in the text you've entered. For instance, you can go back to that extra space and delete it.

2. Move the cursor with the **b,w,h,** *and* **l** *keys in escape mode.*

Use the **b** key to back up the cursor a word at a time. Press **b** enough times to move the cursor to the character just to the right of your extra space. In my example the cursor should be on the **1** of **19** like this:

4/ 19 Scottish dance class

If you move the cursor too many words back with **b,** move it forward one word at a time by pressing the **w** key. When you have the cursor on the letter just to the right of the extra space, press **h** once to move the cursor one character to the left. If you go too far, use the **l** key to move the cursor to the right one character at a time.

3. Delete with **x** *in escape mode.*

When you have the cursor right on the blank space, remove it by pressing the **x** key once. Bingo! The space is gone and the rest of the line moves to the left automatically. In my case, the file now looks like this:

vi
4/14 Put water in the car radiator
4/18 Pay Louise for piano lesson
4/19 Scottish dance class

4. Delete a word with dw
in escape mode, then replace it.

The **x** key removes one character or space. If you want to edit out a word instead of just one space, move the cursor to the first letter of the incorrect word, enter the **dw** (*d*elete *w*ord) command, then use **i** to insert the correct word. For instance, if I had entered this line for April 18 in my calendar file:

4/18 Pay Louise for banana lesson

I would move the cursor to the **b** at the beginning of **banana** as shown, then use the **dw** command to delete that word. After deleting **banana** I could type **i** to go into insert mode, and then enter **piano**.

5. Move the cursor up and down with the k and j
commands in escape mode; delete a line with dd.

If your calendar file is similar to mine, you still have an extra line at the top that says **vi**. To delete it, press the Escape key to get into escape mode, then press the **k** key to move the cursor up. You can press it a number of times to get the cursor all the way up to the top of the file, or you can just hold the key down (this may not work on some terminals). The cursor will go up to the top, then stop there. The terminal will beep at you if you keep pressing the **k** key too long; that means you've gone as far up as you can go. Notice that the cursor moves over to the last character in the **vi** line (the **i**) when it gets up there. Things should look like this:

vi
4/14 Put water in the car radiator
4/18 Pay Louise for piano lesson
4/19 Scottish dance class

To delete the **vi**, press the **d** key twice. The letters disappear. In fact, the whole line disappears, and the rest of the text moves up a line. The cursor is now under the first letter of the first line of calendar dates, like this:

4/14 Put water in the car radiator
4/18 Pay Louise for piano lesson
4/19 Scottish dance class

*A*dding Text to Your vi File

The following procedure tells how to add more lines of text to a file you have begun to create using vi.

1. Use the o *key to open a new line of text.*

If you have just edited a line, and you want to go on to a new line without messing up the one you just fixed, use the **o** key to move the curser to the beginning of the next line and go into insert mode at the same time. For example, if I was up at the top of my calendar file as shown above, I could use the **j** command to move to the beginning of the last line, then use the **o** command, and enter a new line for a future reminder:

> **4/14 Put water in the car radiator**
> **4/18 Pay Louise for piano lesson**
> **4/19 Scottish dance class**
> **4/24 Take out the garbage_**

That's a good one for me. How many Wednesdays have I woken up to the pre-dawn roar of the garbage truck and the clanking of the cans, only to realize that *my* can is not out there for them to pick up? It would be good for me to see that reminder every week.

2. Make a copy of a line using yy *and* p.

If there's something you need to be reminded about once weekly, all you have to do is write the line once, copy it, then change the date. For instance, I can make a copy of my garbage reminder line by using the **yy** command and the **p** command. If I'm at the end of the garbage reminder line, I first press the Escape key, so I'm ready to enter commands. Then I press **y** twice, to "yank" the line into a special place in the computer's memory called a *buffer*. When I hit the **p** key, vi puts the yanked text on the line after the cursor. Here's what I see:

> **4/14 Put water in the car radiator**
> **4/18 Pay Louise for piano lesson**
> **4/19 Scottish dance class**
> **4/24 Take out the garbage**
> **4/24 Take out the garbage**

Notice that you don't get any feedback from vi when you enter the **yy** command. You can't tell where that yanked line went. But you know it's right at hand when you do the **p** command and it appears. If the yanked line didn't appear, and you instead saw the letters **yy** and **p** at the end of the line you meant to copy, you forgot to press the Escape key before you entered those commands. Backspace over the letters to delete them, and then press the Escape key.

If you're ever in doubt as to whether you pressed the Escape key, just hit it again to make sure. It doesn't hurt anything to press the key too often; UNIX just gives you a little beep and lets you go right ahead with your commands.

3. Edit the line you have copied.

In escape mode, use the **l** and **h** keys to move the cursor to a date number you have to change. The **l** key moves the cursor to the right, and **h** moves it back to the left. If you have to change the month as well as the day, as in my example, you don't have to move the cursor with the **l** and **h** keys. When you have the cursor on or under a number you want to change, press the **x** key. The number disappears. Repeat the process for as many numbers as you need to change. To enter the correct date, press **i** for insert, then enter the numbers. In my example, I would press **x** four times, then hit **i** to go into insert mode, then enter **5/1**. So my calendar file would now look like this:

4/14 Put water in the car radiator
4/18 Pay Louise for piano lesson
4/19 Scottish dance class
4/24 Take out the garbage
5/1_Take out the garbage

4. Copy a line into the middle of the file.

If you take a look at the little calendar sample I did, you'll notice that I skipped the garbage reminder for the week of April 17th. If you've made a similar oversight in your calendar, or if you can think of a message you have entered once that you'd like to repeat somewhere else in the middle of your calendar, here's how to do it.

In Escape mode, use the **k** and **j** keys to move the cursor up or down to the line you want to repeat. The cursor doesn't have to be at the beginning or end of the line: anywhere in the line will do. Use **yy** to yank the line. Then move the cursor to the line above where you want the repeated message to appear. Press the **p** key. Bingo, the line is inserted. Now use the **h** and **l** keys to move the cursor to the part of the date that needs changing, **x** out the wrong dates, then hit **i** and enter the correct ones. For instance, in my sample, I would first move the cursor to the 4/24 garbage reminder line, then enter the **yy** command, then press **k** four times to move the cursor up to the top line of my file. Then I would use **p** to put the line in where it belonged, like this:

> **4/14 Put water in the car radiator**
> **4/24 Take out the garbage**
> **4/18 Pay Louise for piano lesson**
> **4/19 Scottish dance class**
> **4/24 Take out the garbage**
> **5/1 Take out the garbage**

Then I'd move the cursor to the **2** of **24**, hit **x** twice, and then press **i** to insert **17**. My calendar would then look like this:

> **4/14 Put water in the car radiator**
> **4/17_Take out the garbage**
> **4/18 Pay Louise for piano lesson**
> **4/19 Scottish dance class**
> **4/24 Take out the garbage**
> **5/1 Take out the garbage**

5. Correct a mistake with u.

Just so you can see how to take care of a mistake in vi, copy a line to the wrong place in the file. Move to the first line of your file with **k**, enter **yy** to yank the line, and then use **j** to move down two lines. Type **p** to put the line in the wrong place. If I do that with my file, I see this:

> **4/14 Put water in the car radiator**
> **4/17 Take out the garbage**
> **4/18 Pay Louise for piano lesson**
> **4/14 Put water in the car radiator**
> **4/19 Scottish dance class**
> **4/24 Take out the garbage**
> **5/1 Take out the garbage**

The important thing to remember, if you make a mistake like this, is not to do anything else until you have used the vi command to undo the mistake.

Now enter **u**. The line disappears, and my file looks like this again:

4/14 Put water in the car radiator
4/17 Take out the garbage
4/18 Pay Louise for piano lesson
4/19 Scottish dance class
4/24 Take out the garbage
5/1 Take out the garbage

The **u** command always *un*does the last thing you did, whatever it was. If you make a mistake like the one above, but type in more text or use another command before you realize it, you can't undo your previous mistake with **u**.

There are other ways to put a misplaced line in its place, though. You can just move the cursor to the line and press **dd** for instance, then go to the line above the place where you want it and type **p**. The line reappears, because **dd** tucks deleted text into the same buffer where the yank command **yy** tucks it. The **p** command takes the text out of that buffer and puts it on the next line.

6. Put several copied lines at the end of the file.

Once you have the idea of yanking and putting lines of text, you can really go to town. You can make a lot of copies of your last line, for instance. Move the cursor to the last line of your file; you can do this with a bunch of **j** commands, or you can take a shortcut and enter **G**. Once you have the cursor on the last line, yank it into the general purpose buffer with the **yy** command. Then use **p** to repeat the line. But hold the **p** key down this time. On most terminals, the line repeats again and again, until it makes the screen scroll upward. If I do it to my file, it looks like Figure 2.2.

As soon as the screen scrolls up six lines, the only thing I can see is repetitions of my 5/1 garbage reminder. While this is a nice demonstration of how quickly one can repeat lines of text in vi, it isn't very useful as it stands. If you copy more lines than you need, just hit **dd** a bunch of times to delete the extras.

```
4/14 Put water in the car radiator
4/17 Take out the garbage
4/18 Pay Louise for piano lesson
4/19 Scottish dance class
4/24 Take out the garbage
5/1 Take out the garbage
5/1 Take out the garbage
5/1 Take out the garbage
5/1 Take out the garbage
5/1 Take out the garbage
5/1 Take out the garbage
5/1 Take out the garbage
5/1 Take out the garbage
5/1 Take out the garbage
```

Figure 2.2: Repeating a line with **p**

Saving Your Work While in vi

When you have done a significant amount of work on a file, you should save it. While you are working on a vi file, or any other file, it is kept in a temporary place in the computer's memory, called the *work buffer*. To save the file permanently on the hard disk in the computer, you have to give a command that tells UNIX to copy the file from the work buffer to the hard disk in the computer.

It's a good idea to save your files to the hard disk pretty often, just in case there's a power surge or some other problem; if the computer shuts down, you might lose all the text for the file that you've typed into the work buffer. If you have saved your file to the hard disk, you can always go back and get it after a power failure or any other mishap. So use the following procedure for saving your work often.

1. Use a colon command to save your file.

First, press the Escape key to make sure you're in escape mode. Then enter : (a colon). Notice that the colon appears down at the bottom of the screen. Then enter **w** (for *w*rite to the hard disk). If I enter the **:w** command, my screen looks like Figure 2.3.

```
  5/1 Take out the garbage
  5/1 Take out the garbage
  5/1 Take out the garbage
  5/1 Take out the garbage
  5/1 Take out the garbage
  5/1 Take out the garbage
  5/1 Take out the garbage
  5/1 Take out the garbage
  5/1 Take out the garbage
  ~
  ~
  ~
  ~
  ~
  ~
  ~
  ~
  ~
  :w_
```

Figure 2.3: *Saving a vi file*

2. Check the write message after saving your file.

When you hit the Return key after entering the **:w** command, a *write message* appears on the bottom line of your screen, stating the name of your new file, how many lines it has in it, and how many characters. After I save my calendar file, my screen looks like Figure 2.4.

```
  5/1 Take out the garbage
  5/1 Take out the garbage
  5/1 Take out the garbage
  5/1 Take out the garbage
  5/1 Take out the garbage
  5/1 Take out the garbage
  5/1 Take out the garbage
  5/1 Take out the garbage
  5/1 Take out the garbage
  ~
  ~
  ~
  ~
  ~
  ~
  ~
  ~
  ~
  "calendar" 81 lines, 2283 characters
```

Figure 2.4: *A write message after saving*

The cursor goes back to the last line of the file, where it was before you entered the colon command. Colon commands let you do something above and beyond the text of your file. After the command is carried out, you're put back in your file, ready to work.

Using Shortcuts in a vi File

Use the following tricks to speed up the process of editing text in vi. These and other time-saving techniques will be covered in more detail in Chapter 9, "Advanced vi."

1. Move to the top of a file with a colon command.

To move to the beginning of your calendar file after saving it, enter **:1** and press the Return key. The first lines of your file appear, with the cursor on the first character of the first line. In my file, things look like this:

```
4/14 Put water in the car radiator
4/17 Take out the garbage
4/18 Pay Louise for piano lesson
4/19 Scottish dance class
4/24 Take out the garbage
5/1 Take out the garbage
5/1 Take out the garbage
5/1 Take out the garbage
5/1 Take out the garbage
5/1 Take out the garbage
5/1 Take out the garbage
```

2. Edit the repeated lines.

Start with the one following the original. In my case, I could hit **j** six times to get down to the line I want to edit. If I wanted to use fewer keystrokes, I could also enter **6j** to move down to that sixth line. Then I would use the **l** twice, **x** out the **1** in the date, and hit **i** so I could insert an **8**. I could do the same sort of editing on the next 3 lines, to make things look like this:

```
4/14 Put water in the car radiator
4/17 Take out the garbage
```

4/18 Pay Louise for piano lesson
4/19 Scottish dance class
4/24 Take out the garbage
5/1 Take out the garbage
5/8 Take out the garbage
5/15 Take out the garbage
5/22 Take out the garbage
5/29 Take out the garbage
5/1 Take out the garbage

To edit the next line, I need to go to the beginning of it and delete **5/1**. I could use **3x** to delete the first three characters, but it wouldn't be much faster than hitting **x** three times. It seems like I'm going to have to do a lot of deleting from this point on, in fact.

3. Repeat a command using . (a period).

If you are going to edit more than a few calendar lines, you'll soon have to delete the month and day entries from them. A good way to do this is to use the **3x** (or **4x** or **5x**, depending on how many digits you have to delete) command, then **j** to go down to the next line, and then enter a period (.). The period repeats the last command that altered text (your delete command). In my case, I would do a **3x**, then press **j**, then . to delete the first three characters in the next line. Then I could just keep pressing **j** and . and clear the first three characters from as many lines as I wanted. If I did it three times, I'd get this:

4/14 Put water in the car radiator
4/17 Take out the garbage
4/18 Pay Louise for piano lesson
4/19 Scottish dance class
4/24 Take out the garbage
5/1 Take out the garbage
5/8 Take out the garbage
5/15 Take out the garbage
5/22 Take out the garbage
5/29 Take out the garbage
Take out the garbage
Take out the garbage
Take out the garbage
_Take out the garbage

Then you can go back and enter the correct month and day for each line. One last trick: to get to the beginning of a line you want to edit, just hit **0** (zero). This takes the cursor directly to the beginning of the line, so you can start inserting the date there. The last four dates look like this:

6/5 Take out the garbage
6/12 Take out the garbage
6/19 Take out the garbage
6/26 Take out the garbage

*A**dding Text to Lines and Between Lines in a vi file***

Use the tricks explained in these steps to put new text into an existing file.

1. Use the A command to add text at the end of a line.

Move the cursor to the line to which you want to add text, using the **k** and **j** keys in escape mode. When the cursor is anywhere on the desired line, enter an **A** (*A*dd). The cursor moves to the first blank space past the end of the existing text, and you are automatically put in insert mode, so you can enter the text you want to add. For instance, if I wanted to add a reminder to the 6/12 line of my calendar file, I'd press the **k** key twice in escape mode to move up there from the last line, then I'd hit **A** and type my addition:

6/5 Take out the garbage
6/12 Take out the garbage, climb Mt.Fuji_
6/19 Take out the garbage
6/26 Take out the garbage

2. Use the a command to add text at the end of a word.

You can add things at the end of a word, rather than at the end of a line. You use a lowercase **a** for this, rather than the **A** command (think of *a* being smaller than *A* just as a word is smaller than a line). For instance, if I wanted to be a little more specific in the line I added, I could go into escape mode, move the cursor to the b at the end of

climb, then hit **a** and add a few words:

6/5 Take out the garbage
6/12 Take out the garbage, climb or crawl up_Mt.Fuji
6/19 Take out the garbage
6/26 Take out the garbage

Because UNIX will eventually read this file to send you daily reminders, don't write a line that's so long it overflows to the next line. UNIX might ignore the overflow when it reads a calendar file. In other vi files, you can type past the end of the line and let vi wrap the text for you.

3. Use the o command to add a new line between two existing lines of text.

Let's say you think of a date to put in your calendar file after you have entered other, later dates. To correct your oversight, move the cursor to the line above where you want to open a new line for a message, then press **o**. The cursor moves down to the beginning of the next line and all the text moves down at the same time, so you have a blank line to fill in with a new date and message. You are also automatically put in insert mode, so you can go right ahead and type the date and message. For example, if I wanted to add an entry for 6/21, I could move the cursor to the 6/19 line, press the **o** key, and type in my reminder so it looked like this:

6/5 Take out the garbage
6/12 Take out the garbage, climb or crawl up Mt.Fuji
6/19 Take out the garbage
6/21 Scottish dance class_
6/26 Take out the garbage

4. Use the O command to open a new line for text at the top of the file.

If you think of a reminder that should appear before the first one in your calendar file, you can just move the cursor to the top of the file, enter **O**, then type the date and message. You can use **k** in escape mode to get to the top line, or you can use the same method you used to get up there and delete the *vi*—:**1**.

When you get to the first line, enter **O** and type in a new message. For instance, I might want to add the following reminder:

4/14 Fix leaky hose for car radiator_
4/14 Put water in the car radiator
4/18 Pay Louise for piano lesson
4/19 Scottish dance class
4/24 Take out the garbage
5/1 Take out the garbage

Notice that there are now two lines with the same date. UNIX won't have any trouble with this when it reads your calendar file. It will just send two reminders on that day.

Finishing Up a vi File

Use the following procedure to look through your vi file for mistakes, fix them, and then save the file and exit vi.

1. Scroll through your file and make finishing touches.

Before you quit working on your first vi file, read it over carefully. If you wrote more than one screenful of text, use the **:1** command in escape mode to get to the first line of the file, then use **Ctrl-f** command to move forward through the text (hold down the Control key and press **f** once). The text will scroll up a single screenful, repeating the last line from the previous screen. If you need to back up a screenful, use **Ctrl-b**.

As you read over your file, look for dates that are incorrect or don't match the month-slash-day format in the samples. If you still have extra lines in your file, move the cursor to them and use **dd** to delete them. If you want to delete several lines, enter a number before the **dd**. For example, if you want to delete 3 extra lines, put the cursor on the first line and enter **3dd**. You can also use the dot command to repeat deletion commands.

2. Save your work and exit vi.

When you have written all the reminders you'll need for the next month or two, or if you have to quit working in vi and go do something else, get into escape mode and enter **ZZ** to exit. A write message appears on the bottom line of your screen, and then the system prompt returns, so the lower part of your screen looks something like Figure 2.5.

```
6/5 Take out the garbage
6/12 Take out the garbage, climb or crawl up Mt Fuji
6/19 Take out the garbage
6/21 Scottish dance class
6/26 Take out the garbage
~
~
~
~
~
~
~
~
~
~
~
~
"calendar" 16 lines, 493 characters
$ _
```

*Figure 2.5: Exiting vi with **ZZ***

If you have to, you could exit vi without saving your file—use the **:q!** command. You can then enter the command **vi calendar** at the shell prompt. When the file appears, it will be the version you last saved.

Congratulations! You have now successfully written a file using vi. It isn't just a useless test file that you'll never see again, either: it's a working calendar file. You can come back and add things to it any time you want, and delete old lines that are outdated.

Using Your Calendar File

You have made a calendar file using vi. Now you can put that file to work. All you have to do is give UNIX the word, and it will take a look at your calendar file every day when you log in. It will send you each reminder message twice: once the day before the date of the reminder, and once on the day you specified.

1. Check to make sure your calendar file is where you left it.

Before you can use the calendar file, you have to make sure UNIX can get at it. To check on this, enter the following command from the system prompt:

```
$ lf
```

The **lf** stands for "list files." When you hit the Return key, UNIX will list the files currently available to you (we'll discuss **lf** in more detail in Chapter 4). There's a good chance that the only file listed will be your calendar file.

2. Tell UNIX to look at your calendar file each time you log in.

To indicate to UNIX that you want to have your calendar file put to use, you have to put the word **calendar** in the start-up file UNIX reads every time you log in. This file is called your *.profile* file. If you use the C-shell on your system (if your system prompt is a **%** instead of a **$**) you have a .login file instead of a .profile file; it looks different, but you do the same thing to it.

First, get into your .profile (or .login) file using vi:

```
$ vi .profile
```

The file will probably look pretty strange. It may have lines like these in it:

```
PATH = /bin:/usr/bin:$HOME/bin:
MAIL = /usr/spool/mail/'logname'
export PATH MAIL
```

It may also have some sort of copyright statement up at the top. Move the cursor to the end of the file with the **G** command. Use **i** to go into insert mode, and write the word **calendar**. Then press the Escape key. If I did that to the sample .profile file shown above, I'd get something like this:

```
PATH = /bin:/usr/bin:$HOME/bin:
MAIL = /usr/spool/mail/'logname'
export PATH MAIL
calendar
```

Use the **ZZ** command to save the change you made to your .profile file and exit vi.

Simple enough, isn't it? You just went right into a file that UNIX uses every time you log in, and edited it so UNIX will do what you want. Using vi in exactly the same way you would use vi on a regular file, you have just made a useful change in the way UNIX behaves when you log in.

This is an extremely important concept in the UNIX world. UNIX gives you access to the files that make it work. You can get right into the nuts and bolts of UNIX, and fix things so that they work the way you want them to. You have a lot of power—this means you can really help (or really hinder) your own work on UNIX. For instance, you have to be careful when you change things in your .profile file; if you change the PATH line, you might end up with some serious difficulties. By carefully adjusting the .profile file, however, you won't do UNIX any harm, and you've enabled it to give you automatic calendar reminders every time you log in. Let's try it out.

3. Log out.

In order to see your calendar reminders for today, log out first. Use **Ctrl-d** or the **logout** command, whichever works on your system.

4. Log in to see today's reminder.

Enter your login name and password to log in again. Enter your terminal type if you are prompted for it. You may see some system messages, but before your system prompt appears, you should see your calendar message for the day. In the sample I wrote for April 14, there were two lines for the day:

```
4/14 Fix leaky hose for car radiator
4/14 Put water in the car radiator
$
```

If you had a reminder in your calendar file for something to do tomorrow, that reminder will also appear—UNIX's way of letting you get a head start on things. UNIX will even go so far as to send you a Monday reminder on the preceding Friday.

5. Delete calendar lines that you no longer need.

After you have received a reminder message for the day, you no longer need the line in your calendar file with that message. Whenever you vi the calendar file to enter new lines for future dates, delete unneeded lines (place the cursor on each line you want to delete, then use the **dd** command to delete it).

Troubleshooting

I don't see the normal vi display.

You are probably in open mode. UNIX tells you this at the bottom of the screen when you use the **vi** command to open a file:

[Using open mode] "calendar" [New file]

This means you are using vi in a mode that only lets you see one line at a time. This is a drag. To get out of open mode, first exit vi by pressing the Escape key and entering the **:q!** command. If you are using the Bourne shell (**$** is your system prompt), enter these commands, hitting the Return key after each one and entering your own terminal type on the second line.

```
cd
TERM = terminal type
export TERM
. .profile
```

Make sure you type the dot and the space before typing **.profile** in the last command. If you see a message like **Terminal type is dumb** or **Terminal type unknown,** try the **. .profile** command again, and make sure you enter your terminal type correctly if you are prompted for it.

If you are using the C-shell (you have a **%** system prompt) enter the following commands instead of the ones shown above:

```
cd
setenv TERM terminal type
source .login
```

You should see a message stating your correct terminal type before your system prompt comes back. If you don't, see your system administrator.

The vi commands don't do anything.

If the command letters appear on the screen, you are probably in insert mode. Hit the Escape key, backspace over the commands and **x** them out, and then try them again while in escape mode.

If things don't work any better when you're in escape mode, either the terminal or the computer is missing some cues. First check your Caps Lock and Alpha Lock keys to make sure they aren't pressed down. If everything seems all right, and you still can't get your commands to register, see your system administrator.

My system prompt reappeared.

You have accidentally entered a key sequence that sends you back to UNIX. If you have just been sent back temporarily, most systems give you a **:sh** at the bottom of your screen before your system prompt appears. This means that the keys you hit by accident have the same effect as the colon command, **sh**. The **sh** command is not a rude way of telling UNIX to hush, but a quick request for a *sh*ell. It's a bit like interrupting a conversation at your table to order something extra from a waiter in the UNIX cafe. (For more information on this sort of request, see "Colon Commands" in Chapter 9.) To get back into your calendar file with vi, just type **exit** at the system prompt and press the Return key. You'll go right back to the calendar file where you left it.

If neither of these does the job, you may have accidentally quit vi by pressing **ZZ** in escape mode.

I can't exit vi.

First make sure you are in escape mode. Hit the Escape key and wait a few seconds. Something may have slowed the system down. If the terminal beeps when you press the Escape key, you are ready to give your exit command (for example, **ZZ**).

When I logged out and logged in again, the reminder message didn't appear.

First check the date in your calendar file to make sure it is today's date, and that it is in the form month/day, as shown in the samples. If the date is correct, it may be that the messages in your calendar file are not being read by UNIX. The calendar file must be readable by all users so UNIX can read them, too. To set up your file so it can be read by all users, see the section on permissions in Chapter 4.

Command Summary

COMMAND	DESCRIPTION
filename	Starts vi and opens file with specified name.

COMMANDS IN VI

i	Lets you insert text at cursor postition.
o	Lets you open a new line for text below the cursor.
O	Lets you open a new line for text above the cursor.
a	Lets you add text to the right of the cursor.
A	Lets you add text at the end of the line the cursor is on.
Escape (Esc)	Puts you in escape mode from insert mode.
x	Deletes one character.
dw	Deletes one word.
dd	Deletes one line.
u	Undoes the last text-altering command.
j	Moves the cursor down one line.
k	Moves the cursor up one line.
l	Moves the cursor one character to the right.
h	Moves the cursor one character to the left.
w	Moves the cursor forward (to the right) one word.
b	Moves the cursor back (to the left) one word.
Ctrl-F	Moves the cursor forward one screenful.
Ctrl-B	Moves the cursor back one screenful.
yy	Yanks a line of text.
p	Puts last yanked or deleted text after cursor.
ZZ	Saves file and exits vi.

COMMAND   DESCRIPTION

COLON COMMANDS IN VI

:1   Moves cursor to first line in file.

:w   Writes (saves) file to the hard disk.

:q!   Exits vi without saving last changes to file.

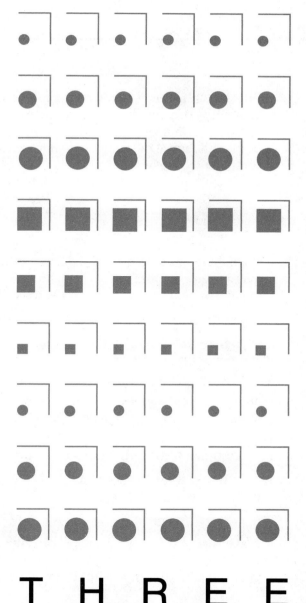

T H R E E

**Using
Electronic
Mail**

Electronic mail is one of the most useful aspects of multi-user computing. If your terminal is connected to a computer that has several other terminals connected to it, you can exchange "email" messages with several other users. If your computer is connected to other computers to make a network, and your network to other networks, you may be able to send electronic mail to millions of other users.

UNIX tells you when you have gotten a message in the mail with a message something like this:

You have new mail.

If you have just logged in for the first time on your UNIX system, you may not have any mail yet. You can, however, send some e-mail messages to yourself, and learn how to write and send e-mail in the process.

Sending an E-mail Message

To send an e-mail message, you address it to a user, write the message, then send it off. In the following procedure, use your own login name in order to send a message to yourself.

1. Use the mail command to address your message.

If you want to mail yourself a letter, enter the following command, using your own login name where shown:

$ mail *loginname*

Make sure you type your name correctly; the mail program is very particular about addresses. When you press the Return key, the mail program asks you for a subject. For me, it looks like this:

**$ mail tomc
Subject:**

2. Enter a subject for your email message.

You can specify the subject of your message any way you want, but it's good to write short, clear subjects for your email messages. When a message is sent, the subject of the message appears on a list of messages to that person, so that he or she can see what each one is about. In this case, you'll be sending several messages to yourself, so you should give each one a name that sets it apart, like:

$ mail tomc
Subject: trial message A

When you hit return, the cursor goes to the next line and waits for your input.

3. Get into vi to write your message.

You could start typing the mail message now, using the simple text editor that comes with the mail program. But since you already know how to use vi, you should use it here—it's much more versatile than the mail message text editor. To get into vi, type ˜**v**, like this:

$ mail tomc
subject: trial message A
˜ v

You will see the familiar vi screen, with the tildes (˜) running down the left margin. You'll also see a note at the bottom of the screen that says something like this:

"/tmp/Re09907" 0 lines, 0 characters

This means that you're writing a temporary vi file that will soon become a mail message.

4. Enter the text of your message.

You can write anything you want in this first message, but try to write at least three or four lines. If you aren't feeling inspired, you can copy the text of the following sample message:

Tom -
You too can learn to send e-mail messages. Once you
address a message and write a subject, you can enter vi and
use all the editing methods you have learned already. For
more information on this exciting subject, just email five
dollars and a self-addressed stamped envelope to...
- Tom :-)

The odd little symbol at the end of the letter is an *emoticon,* incidentally. Tip your head to the left to see what emotion the emoticon "face" is supposed to convey. This one means "take the preceding with a smile." You may see various emoticons if you read network news.

5. Quit vi and use Ctrl-d to send the message.

When you are done with your message, press the Escape key and type **ZZ** to quit vi. A message appears at the bottom of the screen telling you that a temporary file has been created. Below it, there's a polite request prompting you to continue with your mailing. Things should look something like this:

"/tmp/Rel14400" 10 lines, 297 characters
(continue)

—

If you are satisfied with the message you have written, just press **Ctrl-d** at this point, and the mail program will close your message and prepare it for mailing. In effect, you are "logging out" of the little shell—your message—to get back into a bigger shell—your account. Hence you use the same command here to get out of your message as you do on many systems to log out of UNIX entirely. Entering a period (.) may also work on many UNIX systems. If you decide the whole letter was a mistake and you want to avoid sending it, just press the Delete key twice.

If you close your message with either **Ctrl-d** or a period, the next thing you see is a **Cc:** prompt, asking you who you want to send carbon copies of your mail message to.

6. Specify to whom you want to send carbon copies.

If you have written an important message that you want other people on your UNIX system to see, type in their login names. Make sure you never enter more text for your message at the **Cc:** prompt; the mail program will reject it.

If you're sending a dumb little test message to yourself like the one above, and don't want to send copies to anybody, just hit the Returnkey at the **Cc:** prompt. You'll know your message is on its merry way when you see an end-of-message statement, and your system prompt returns:

(end of message)
$

You have sent your first message—good work. As long as the address (your login name) was correct, you ought to get it in your electronic mailbox soon. On some systems, a notification message will appear on your screen, just like the one you see if you have mail when you log in. If you see the notification, you'll know for sure that your message is in your mailbox. Before reading it, though, send a few more for practice.

If you make a mistake in spelling your login name, the message doesn't reach anyone. Instead, you get a **mail problem** message from the "mailer daemon" (the program responsible for delivering mail). For example, if I try to send mail to **tgmc** instead of **tomc**, my message from the mailer daemon says:

No local user named tgmc

Don't get too concerned if this happens to you: the mail daemon isn't going to come after your soul if you make a mistake. Use the ‾ **M** command, discussed later in this chapter, to resend the mail message.

7. Mail yourself three more short messages for practice.

Try the whole procedure again a few times. For each message, enter: **mail** *loginname*, and then enter a subject (like **trial message B, trial message C**, and **trial message D**). After entering the subject, just hit the ‾ **v** to get into vi, then type a few words for a message (like **This is trial B** for message B). Then press the Escape key and enter **ZZ** to get out of vi, and type **Ctrl-d** when mail asks you to continue. Press the Return key at the **Cc:** prompt, and the message will be sent. When you have sent a number of messages, you're ready to start learning about the receiving end of e-mail.

Reading Your E-mail and Disposing of Messages

To read your mail, all you have to do is give the **mail** command at the system prompt and select a message to read. Once you have read through a message, you can do a number of things with it. The following procedure describes your e-mail options in detail.

1. Start the mail program and view your message list.

To start mail and see a list of the messages that you have received, enter **mail** at the system prompt. A short statement about the mail program appears, with a hint about how to get help if you need it. Below this information line there is a line stating how many messages you have. The top two lines of text on your screen look something like this:

mail version 3.0 January 28, 1987. Type ? for help.
5 messages

A message list follows. The messages appear in the order they were received, usually with the most recent message at the top. For each message, the following information is displayed: the message number, the sender, the date and time the message was sent, the number of lines and characters in the message, and the subject. The screen looks like Figure 3.1.

```
$  mail
mail version 3.0 January 28, 1987.  Type ? for help.
5 messages:
    1 lorim     Fri Jun 16 12:48  11/186 "timesheet approved"
    2 tomc      Fri Jun 16 13:37  16/399 "trial message A"
    3 tomc      Fri Jun 16 15:17  7/118  "trial message B"
    4 tomc      Fri Jun 16 15:22  7/118  "trial message C"
    5 tomc      Fri Jun 16 15:25  7/118  "trial message D"

&  _
```

Figure 3.1: Your e-mail message list

Under the message list is a new mail program cursor, an ampersand (&). On some systems, the prompt may be a question mark or a double line (the lower part of the double line blinks, if your usual system cursor blinks). You still use the prompt in the same way as the system prompt, though—the change is just so you don't forget you're inside the mail program.

You'll notice one difference between your message list and mine; I have a message at the top of my list that isn't one I sent to myself. My boss, Lori, has approved my timesheet, so I'll get paid soon. You may have a letter or two from other users in your message list, too. Don't worry about them for now. They're safe in your system mailbox until you read them and decide what to do with them. Even if you quit mail, messages you haven't looked at stay in your system mailbox until you start mail again and read them.

2. Select the number of a message to read it.

To read a mail message, all you have to do is enter its number at the mail prompt and press Return. For instance, if I want to see message 2, the first trial message I sent to myself, I can enter **2**. The mail program responds by showing me the message, as you can see in Figure 3.2. (Depending on how long your message is, you may still be able to see part of the message list at the top of your screen.)

```
2
Message 2:
From tomc Fri Jun 16 13:37:02 1991
To: tomc
Subject: trial message A
Date: Fri Jun 16 13:37:01 1991

Tom -
You too can learn to send email messages.
Once you address a message and write a
Subject, you can enter vi and use all the
editing methods you have learned already.
For more information on this exciting
subject, just email five dollars and a
self-adressed stamped envelope to...
- Tom :-)
```

Figure 3.2: *A sample e-mail message*

Mail displays several lines of information about the message before the text of the message. These lines are called the "header." In the example shown, the header tells me the message number, who the message is from, when I received it, who it was addressed to, what the subject is, and when it was sent. The header information is all pretty obvious in this sample. But some messages can have more interesting headers. For instance, if the message was sent to a group of people, you might see all of their names in the **To:** line, or in the **Cc:** line.

If the text of a message is long, the mail program should show you just the first 20 lines or so, and display a question mark prompt at the bottom of the screen. Press the Return key to see the next 20 lines of the message. If long messages scroll too quickly for you to read them, see the "Troubleshooting" section at the end of this chapter.

When you get to the end of a message you're reading, the question mark prompt goes away, and you see the mail (ampersand) prompt again. If you want to reread the message, enter **p** at the mail prompt.

3. Decide whether to delete or save the message.

The mail cursor waits at the end of your message until you decide what to do with it. I'm going to delete this one. If you want to save your first message, go on to step 6.

4. Delete messages
with the d or dp command, undelete with u.

To delete the message you just read, enter **d** at the mail prompt. This takes your message out of the list, but it doesn't erase it until you quit the mail program. If you decide you want the letter after all, and you're still in mail, you can enter **u** and it'll come back.

If you delete several messages, then decide to undelete one of them, you have to tell mail which one. For example, if you deleted message 2, read and deleted message 3, and then decided you needed to undelete message 2 after all, you would have to enter **u 2** to get message 2 back.

Multiple messages can be specified in different ways. You can enter several numbers with a space between each. For example, **d 1 3** means to delete messages 1 and 3. You can also delete a range of messages: **d 1-3** deletes messages 1, 2, and 3. This works with many mail commands which take message numbers as an argument.

You can also delete a message straight out of the message list without reading it, by specifying a message number after **d** in the same way. If, for example, I wanted to delete that timesheet message without reading it (the subject line says it all), I would enter the following command at the mail prompt:

d 1

If you are reading through your mail list and want to delete a message you just read, and then immediately go on to read the next one, enter **dp** and hit the Return key. Don't try using the **d** command and pressing Return twice to delete a letter and read the next one. It doesn't work; mail skips the next message and shows you the one after it instead. If you do this all the way through your mail list, you leave half of it unread.

5. Use the h command to see the message list again.

Whenever the mail cursor appears at the end of a message or after you have entered a mail command, you can enter **h** and take a look at the message list to see what has happened. For example, if you delete messages 1 and 2, then press **h**, the list looks like Figure 3.3.

```
d 2
h
1 lorim      Fri  Jun  16  12:48  11/186  "timesheet approved"
3 tomc       Fri  Jun  16  15:17   7/118  "trial message B"
4 tomc       Fri  Jun  16  15:22   7/118  "trial message C"
5 tomc       Fri  Jun  16  15:25   7/118  "trial message D"
```

Figure 3.3: *Message list with one message deleted*

The sample shown is a short list. If you need to hunt through a long list, you could use the **h +** and **h-** variants of the **h** command to hunt farther down the list or farther up.

But as for the list above, with messages 1 and 2 deleted, if I enter **u 2** at the mail prompt, then **h** again, message 2 appears back in the list. I could select message 2 and view it again if I wanted to make sure it wasn't deleted. (I really don't want to see my message 2 again, so I'm going to leave it in deletion limbo.)

6. Save a message in your mailbox with the mb command.

If you have a message that's worth saving, the easiest way to save it is to enter the **mb** command at the end of the message. This command puts the message in a special place called the **mbox** file.

For example, I could select message 3 from my message list, and enter **mb** at the mail prompt after I'm done reading it. Then, if I gave the **h** command to look at my message list, I'd see an **M** next to message 3, as shown in Figure 3.4. The **M** indicates the message is marked for saving to the mbox file.

```
    1 lorim     Fri Jun 16 12:48 11/186 "timesheet approved"
M 3 tomc      Fri Jun 16 15:17 7/118  "trial message B"
    4 tomc      Fri Jun 16 15:22 7/118  "trial message C"
    5 tomc      Fri Jun 16 15:25 7/118  "trial message D"
```

Figure 3.4: Message list with one message marked for mbox

You can save as many messages as you want in this file. When you want to read one again, use the mail program to list them and select the one you're interested in, as described later in this chapter.

7. Save a message to a file with the s filename command.

If you save all your mail messages in the mbox file, it gets overloaded pretty fast. It's better to save messages to different files, so you can find old messages on a given subject easily. You may not know yet what categories you want in your mail file library, but you can still save one of your trial messages to a file. In my sample message list, for instance, I could select message 4, read it, and then enter this command at the mail prompt:

s tests

When I press the Return key, the mail program tells me that it saved my message into a new file called *tests,* containing a certain number of lines and characters. In my sample, the mail program's response is:

"tests" [New file] 7/118

If you save other messages to this file later, mail appends them to the file, leaving the first message there. You can read these saved messages just as if you were reading mail freshly received; see "Reading a Mail File from the System Prompt" later in this chapter.

When you save a message, then display the message list with the **h** command, the saved messages appear with an asterisk before them, as shown in Figure 3.5.

You can also save messages to your mbox with the **s** command without any filename. This works just like the **mb** command.

```
    1 lorim     Fri Jun 16 12:48 11/186 "timesheet approved"
M 3 tomc        Fri Jun 16 15:17 7/118 "trial message B"
* 4 tomc        Fri Jun 16 15:22 7/118 "trial message C"
    5 tomc      Fri Jun 16 15:25 7/118 "trial message D"
```

Figure 3.5: *Message list with asterisk by saved message*

8. Use the ho command
to hold a message in the system mailbox.

If you have to stop reading your mail and quit the program before you've finished reading all the messages, you can keep them in the system mailbox, so they'll be there next time you read your mail. Don't hold messages in the system mailbox unless you have to, though. It puts a burden on the whole email system to leave messages in it.

If you need to hold just a message or two, enter the command **ho** *n* (where *n* is a message number) from the mail prompt. For example, to hold message number 5 in my sample list, I would enter **ho 5** and press the Return key. On most mail systems, you see an **H** or a **P** next to each unread message you hold for later reading. My sample list, if I hold message 5, looks like Figure 3.6.

```
    1 lorim     Fri Jun 16 12:48 11/186 "timesheet approved"
M 3 tomc        Fri Jun 16 15:17 7/118 "trial message B"
* 4 tomc        Fri Jun 16 15:22 7/118 "trial message C"
H 5 tomc        Fri Jun 16 15:25 7/118 "trial message D"
```

Figure 3.6: *Message list with H by the message to be held*

If your mail program does not automatically save messages you have read to your mbox, no **H** or **P** appears in the list by the held messages. That's OK; if you don't have auto-mbox, unread messages as well as read ones are automatically held in the system mailbox.

Replying to Mail

If you want to respond to a message after reading it, use the following procedure to make a reply.

1. Use the r or R command to reply to a mail message.

If you have just finished reading a message, type **r** to reply to the sender, or **R** to respond to the sender and send a copy of your response to all the users copied in the message that came to you. Don't use the **R** command unless you are really sure all the people on that **Cc:** list would be interested in your response.

You can respond to a message directly from the message list by entering the **r** *n* command. If I wanted to thank Lori for approving my timesheet, for instance, I could enter **r 1** when looking at the message list, or simply **r** at the mail prompt that appears when I finish reading message 1. In either case, the following header is displayed:

To: lorim
Subject: timesheet approved

The cursor appears below the subject, ready for you to enter your response.

A note to users who do not have SCO UNIX; the functions of **r** and **R** might be reversed in your mail program.

2. Incorporate the message in your reply with ˜ m.

If you want to put the contents of the message you are replying to into your response, so the sender will be reminded of what you are replying to, enter the ˜ **m** command on the first line of your reply, before going into vi. You see a little note, like this:

Interpolating: 1
(continue)

The cursor appears on a new line, ready for you to enter your reply.

3. Use vi to enter your reply.

Enter the ˜ **v** command to go into vi. The message appears, header and all, indented from the usual margin:

> **From lorim Fri Jun 16 12:48:05 1991**
> **To: tomc**
> **Subject: timesheet approved**
> **Date: Fri Jun 16 12:49:30 1991**
>
> **Your timesheet for the week ending Jun 16 has been approved.**

As usual, a note about a temporary file appears at the bottom of the screen. The cursor appears at the top line of the included message. You can now add your response.

4. Use the O command to enter text before the included message.

With the cursor at the top line of the included message, use the **O** command to go into insert mode, opening a line for your text above the included message. You can write a short introductory line here. For example, I could say:

> **In regards to your message:**
>
> —
> **From lorim Fri Jun 16 12:48:05 1991**
> **To: tomc**
> **Subject: timesheet approved**
> **Date: Fri Jun 16 12:49:30 1991**
>
> **Your timesheet for the week ending Jun 16 has been approved.**

Press Return after you finish your introductory line. A blank line will open up between what you wrote and the included message, as shown. This blank line will visually offset the message you're including from your own.

5. Use the G and o commands to enter text after the included message.

As you recall from your vi practice, you can move the cursor to the end of the included message quickly if you go into escape mode and press **G**. The cursor will probably appear on a blank line below the last line of the included message. Enter **o** to go into insert mode on the next line, leaving a blank line to set off the included message, as before. You can put your reply before the included message, rather than after it, or you can even put comments in the middle of the included letter. But if you enter a short reply after the message, you'll wind up with something like this:

Lori - In regards to your message:

> **From lorim Fri Jun 16 12:48:05 1991**
> **To: tomc**
> **Subject: timesheet approved**
> **Date: Fri Jun 16 12:49:30 1991**
>
> **Your timesheet for the week ending Jun 16 has been approved.**

Thanks for approving my hours so quickly. Payroll said I'd be able to pick up my check on Wednesday, so I'll have money when I leave for NY Thursday after all. I'm grateful for your extra effort.
- Tom _

Although it isn't required, it's a good idea to address the person you're responding to at the beginning of your reply, and to sign off with your name at the end of the reply. In cases where e-mail is forwarded two or three times, signing off helps future readers identify who wrote what.

6. Exit vi, then send your reply with Ctrl-d.

When you have finished your reply and signed off, go into escape mode and use the **ZZ** command to exit from vi. You'll see the familiar note about your temporary vi file, and an invitation to continue with the mailing process. Just enter **Ctrl-d** at this point, then hit the Return key at the **Cc:** prompt, and your reply will be sent to the person who wrote to you. The **(end of message)** note appears, and then the ampersand mail prompt.

Other Mail Functions

The following hints will help you make full use of electronic mail.

Save helpful hints by writing messages to yourself.

If you learn some new trick for using the UNIX system and you don't want to forget it, mail it in a message to yourself, and keep all such messages in a single file. For example, you could send yourself a message with the subject **Saving hints in mail file** and then save the message in a file called **hints**. You could add all the helpful hints messages to the hints file, both your own and ones other users mail to you. Then, when you can't remember a hint, use the **mail -f** command, as described later in this chapter, to list all your hint messages. Message headings are much easier to look through than a list of cryptic filenames.

Forward mail with the f n loginname *command.*

When you are looking at the message list, you can forward any message you have received to another user. Just type **f**, a space, the message number, another space, and the login name of the person you want to forward the message to. The mail program tells you the message has been forwarded. If you make a mistake in writing the person's login name, you will get a message in your mail from the "mailer daemon" saying that the message could not be delivered. If this happens, just forward it again and make sure you get the login name spelled right.

Print a mail message with the l n *command.*

When viewing the message list, you can print out a message by entering l (lowercase L, not the number one), a space, and the message number. When you press the Return key, a short note appears, saying which message was sent to the printer. It is followed by a "request id" message, which you don't really have to worry about. It just means your request to print something has gone to the print spooler, which keeps all print requests in order until they can go to the printer. The name of the printer (often abbreviated, just to keep things cryptic) appears in the message, as well as a description of the type of input you're sending. For instance, if I send message 12 to my printer, which is called "lab," I see the following messages:

Messages sent to line printer: 12
request id is lab-7428 (standard input)

Your print job may have to wait in line for a while, but if the printer is in working order and there aren't many jobs waiting in front of yours, you should be able to go pick up your message at the printer in a few minutes.

Send blind carbon copies
or to get a return-receipt for a message you are writing.

When you are writing a message you can modify the header that appears at the top of it. Either before or after you enter vi to write the text of your message, enter the ˜h command. Each line of the header is displayed, including a blind carbon copy line and a line for a return receipt message. If I used the ˜h command when I was writing my first trial message, I would see something like this:

To: tomc
Subject: trial message A
Cc:
Bcc:
Return-receipt-to: tomc

The Blind carbon copy line is for copying people privately. Enter the login names of the people you want to send copies to (without knowing who else is getting a copy) in the **Bcc:** line. Put your own name in the **Return-receipt-to:** line if you want to know if your message has reached the system mailbox of the person you addressed it to. This is valuable if you send an urgent message that the addressee must get within a limited time. Sometimes mail takes a while to deliver messages, especially if your UNIX system is part of a network and the network is having problems.

Include a file in your message with the ˜ r command.

If you want to mail a file to another user, address a message to them, and after writing an introductory note, use the ˜ r command to read the file into your mail message. Beware of sending files with special characters; the mail program cannot convey many of these characters. But all standard text files can be sent via mail. For instance, I could send my calendar file to myself as follows:

```
$ mail tomc
Subject: calendar
Here is my calendar file:
˜ r calendar
```

The mail program would then respond with a short note saying something like **"calendar" 36/654**. This note tells me the calendar file, which has 36 lines and 654 characters, is now included in my message. If you want to see an included file, just use the ˜ v command to look at it in vi.

Use the ˜ M command
to resend mail returned by the mailer daemon.

If you get a "mail problem" message from the mail program and it contains a long message that you sent, you can resend the message. If you make a mistake entering the login name of an addressee, or if mail returns a message for some other reason, you don't have to rewrite the message. Just use the **mail** command with the correct login name and enter the subject you entered on the original message. Then, instead of going directly into vi, enter ˜ **M** *n*, substituting the number of the message from the mailer daemon for *n*. After you see the "interpolating" note, go into vi. The message from the daemon appears, with your returned message at the end of it. Delete all the lines of the daemon's message, then exit from vi, use **Ctrl-d** to close the message, and resend it to the correct login address.

Exiting Mail

When you have read all your messages and either deleted or saved them, exit mail by entering **q** at the mail prompt. A note appears, telling you how many messages, if any, are left in your system mailbox, and how many messages have been saved in your **mbox** file. For example, if I read all of my mail, deleted all the messages (after saving the ones I wanted to keep into the appropriate files), and saved one message in my **mbox** file, I would see:

Held 0 messages in /usr/spool/mail/tomc
Saved 1 message in /u/tomc/mbox
$ _

Your system prompt returns, as shown.

Reading a Mail File from the System Prompt

If you have saved mail messages to files, you can use the mail program to list them, read them and do anything else with them that you can do with a mail message you have just received. For instance, I can look at the mail messages I have saved to the file **tests** by using the following command:

$ mail -f tests

When you hit the Return key, you see a line of information about the mail program, then the list of messages in that file. In my sample there's only one file, so the list is short:

mail version 3.0 January 28, 1987 Type ? for help.
1 message:
1 tomc   Fri Jun 16 15:22 7/118 "trial message A"

If you save a bunch of messages to the same file, they all appear in the list, which makes it very easy to find a message you saved a long time ago and forgot about.

Troubleshooting

Long mail messages go by so fast I can't read them.

See your UNIX User's Reference to learn how to set your own page length, as described in the "Customizing Your email" section of

Chapter 10, or see your system administrator and request to have the page length set for reading mail.

I can't remember a user's login name.

If your UNIX system has an on-line directory, try entering **ext** at the system prompt, a space, and then your best guess at the user's login name or full name. If the on-line directory is a good one, it'll give you a list of existing login names that are close to your guess.

If you don't have an on-line directory of users, try the **who** command and see if the user is logged in. If that doesn't work, get a hard-copy directory of the users on your system. It's a good idea to have one of these anyway—especially if you have a big UNIX system with dozens (perhaps hundreds) of users.

I can't remember a mail command.

If you are reading mail, get to the end of a message (press Return until you see the mail cursor). Then type a **?** and press Return again.

If you are writing a message, move the cursor to the beginning of a new line, then enter a **˜?** and press the Return key.

In either case, a list of mail commands appears, with a short explanation of each command.

Command Summary

COMMAND	DESCRIPTION
READING MAIL:	
n	Reads specified message.
d *n*	Deletes specified message.*
dp	Deletes current message, and then reads the next message.
f *n loginname*	Forwards specified message to user *loginname.**
h	Lists one screenful of mail headers.
h+	Lists next screenful of mail headers.

COMMAND	DESCRIPTION

READING MAIL:

h −	Lists previous screenful of mail headers.
h *loginname*	Lists messages from a person.
ho *n*	Holds specified message in system mailbox.*
l *n*	Prints specified message.*
mb *n*	Saves specified message in your mbox file.*
p	Displays last message.
q	Quits mail and deletes marked messages.
r *n*	Allows you to reply to specified message.*
s *n filename*	Saves specified message to a file.*
u *n*	Undeletes specified message.*
x	Quits mail and leaves messages in system mailbox.
?	Lists mail commands.

WRITING MAIL:

˜h	Allows you to edit headers and add Blind Cc or Return Receipt.
˜m *n*	Includes specified message, indented, in the message you are writing.
˜M *n*	Includes specified message, unindented.
˜r *filename*	Includes specified file in your message.
˜v	Puts you into vi.
˜?	Lists mail commands without exiting current message.
Ctrl-d	Ends message; gives you Cc prompt.
Delete	When pressed twice, discontinues message.

*If no message number (*m*) is entered, the command takes effect on the current message.

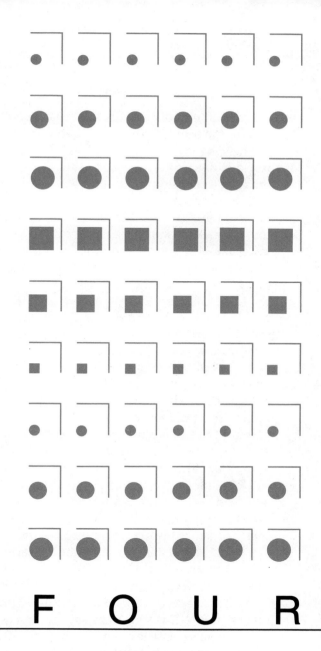

F O U R

**Learning about
Files and Directories**

Lincoln said government should be "of the people, by the people, for the people." Thompson and Ritchie designed UNIX to be "of the files, by the files, for the files." Everything you do in the UNIX world is done with files. For instance, when you start the mail program, you are using a file; when you save a message in mail, it is saved in a file. Even the errors you make in sending messages are kept in a file. And files are used to display everything you see on your terminal, too. It's hard to explain files in terms of the UNIX cafe, but you might say that everything used to order, prepare, contain, serve, and eat the meal, from the waiter's pencil to the ten-burner kitchen stove to your salad fork, are all files.

These files are all kept in *directories*. Directories are like the folders used to hold paper files in a file cabinet. The difference is that you can put directories as well as files inside a directory. There is almost no limit to how many directories and files you can have inside any one directory; all of the directories in your UNIX system are in a single, "root" directory.

In the real world, if you put a folder full of files in a second folder, then put that second folder with a bunch of other folders and files in a third folder, and put *that* folder with a bunch of other folders and files in a fourth folder, then the folder holding everything else gets so big and bulky you can't manage it. This is not the case in the world of UNIX files and directories; you can have many layers of directories and files. As long as it is all organized in a clear hierarchy, it is pretty easy to manage. But you have to understand the hierarchy to keep things organized when you make your own files and directories.

That's what this chapter is about; learning how files and directories are organized on your UNIX system, and how to keep your own files organized in directories so you can find them quickly and easily. There is also a section on limiting access to private files. This is important in the UNIX world. Since any user can explore any part of the file system, you need to have a way to limit the files other users can look at and change in your own directories.

Taking a Tour of the File System

If you want to learn how the files and directories of your UNIX system are organized, take a look around the file system for yourself.

The file system is the whole organization of files and directories. Start at your home base, and take a look at the directories and files that are important to you.

1. Use the pwd *command to see where you are in the file system.*

If you enter **pwd** at the system prompt, UNIX tells you which directory you are in. The letters stand for *p*rint *w*orking *d*irectory; that means display on your screen the directory you are working in. If you have logged in and you haven't changed into some other directory, you'll see that your working directory has your login name, unless you have some kind of customized login setup. For me, the output of **pwd** looks like this:

/u/tomc

It makes sense that the directory you start working in when you log in is named after you. In fact, the directory with your name is called your "home" directory because it is where you start out in the UNIX file system.

But what about those slash signs and the letter **u** that appear before your name? They tell you where your home directory is in the file system. They describe a path from the "root" or topmost directory, the one that contains all the others, down to your home directory. Your home directory is inside the /u directory, and the /u directory is inside the root directory. The name of the root directory is slash. That's why the first thing in the path is a slash. The other slash is a divider between the /u directory and your home directory. You'll see lots of slashes between directory and file names in paths, but the first one in each path, if it appears before any of the names, always refers to the root directory. If you have worked with a DOS file system, you have seen backslashes (\) used as dividers in pathnames. The concept in UNIX is similar. (Just to make things a little more complicated, it's convention to put a slash in front of a directory name. We write "the /u directory" instead of "the u directory.")

Some file systems may have a /usr directory instead of a /u directory like I have. But on most systems, the users' home directories are inside a directory with a name that's one abbreviation of "user" or another, and this user directory is inside the root directory.

To get an idea of what the **pwd** command showed me about the file system, think of an upside-down tree, with the / (root) directory at the top, the /u directory under the root directory on one of its branches, and my home directory, /tomc , under the /u directory, on one of the twigs that grow down from the branch. Figure 4.1 shows a sample file system "tree."

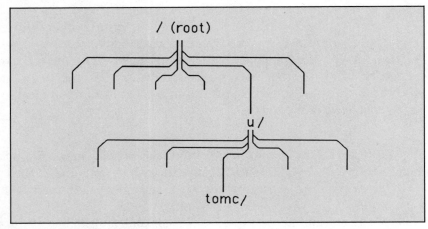

Figure 4.1: *A file system tree*

Can you see how the information that the **pwd** command gave you in horizontal form appears in the vertical order of the directory tree? Notice that the directories other than root have slashes after them. That's another UNIX custom. It lets you know that what you're looking at is a directory and not a plain file. That makes sense—more sense than an upside-down tree, at any rate. Why they didn't do it right-side-up is beyond me, but that's the way everybody draws directory trees, so we have to go along with it. The UNIX world does have its own, quirky sense of order, and it's a good thing to remember that some things are going to seem upside-down until you get used to them.

2. Use the If command to see what's in your home directory.

The **lf** command *lists files* in your working directory. If you find that **lf** doesn't work on your system, use **ls -f** instead. When you list the files in your home directory one way or the other, you will see the names of the files running across your screen. My list looks like this:

calendar   hints   mbox   tests

Recognize those files? There's the calendar file I made in Chapter 2, and the mbox tests and hints files I made by saving mail messages in Chapter 4. You probably have files with different names. If I add my files to my UNIX file system tree, it looks like Figure 4.2.

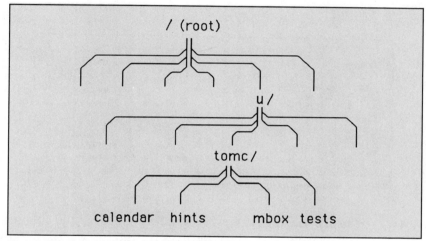

Figure 4.2: *A home directory in a file system tree*

3. Move to the directory above with the cd .. command.

To get to the directory immediately above your home directory, use the **cd ..** (*c*hange *d*irectory) command, and make sure you enter a space before the periods. The two periods together mean "directory above" the working directory. This is a *relative* command; it moves you in relation to your current position. When you press the Return key after entering the command correctly, your system prompt appears, but you get no other hint that anything has changed. Use the **pwd** command to check where you are.

You'll see **/u** if your file system is like mine. You'll see **/usr** or **/user** if your file system has one of those directories instead of a /u directory. From now on, I'll just refer to the /u directory, so if you have one of those other ones, substitute it for /u in the file system.

4. List the files in this directory with the lf command.

Just enter **lf** and look at the listing. The first thing you'll notice is that **lf** lists directories as well as files. That's because a directory is seen as a special type of file in the UNIX file system. The only difference between a plain file and a directory file, as far as UNIX is concerned, is that a directory file can have more files and directories inside it, and a plain file can't. The listing of the /u directory on my system is shown in Figure 4.3.

```
allani/      caroll/      ericx/       jonm/        mikeg/       sysadm/
anag/        claudem/     galeg/       josephi/     naomic/      tammys/
angelam/     dank/        gaylel/      katei/       peggye/      teresaf/
appts/       davex/       georgei/     keiths/      ravenc/      teric/
arthurf/     davidc/      hannao/      kellyc/      ricke/       tims/
artp/        davidk/      heather/     kevinx/      robertc/     tomc/
backup/      davidw/      jamesd/      lindah/      scadm/       vickic/
bartb/       dennisn/     jimk/        lorim/       stanc/       zursh/
billq/       diannaq/     joani/       lost+found/  stephant/
bin/         docadm/      joee/        marku/       steven/
bobt/        ericm/       johnw/       megn/        stewartd/
```

Figure 4.3: A sample /u directory listing

The files and directories are listed alphabetically, in columns. In this /u directory, all of the listed files are directory files, so they all have slashes after them.

Most of the directories in Figure 4.3 are users on my system. Your /u directory may not be so crowded; you may or may not see directories like /bin and /lost + found in your /u directory. There's no rule that says the user directory can only have users in it. On some systems, there are lots of things other than users in there. Most of the time there aren't any plain files in the directory, but even that convention gets broken in some cases. If we put some of these user directories in their place in the directory tree, we get Figure 4.4.

You can imagine the other user directories spreading far out to the left of the figure. If you imagine all the files that all those directories contain branching out under the directories like my files are in the picture, you begin to see just how big a UNIX file system can be.

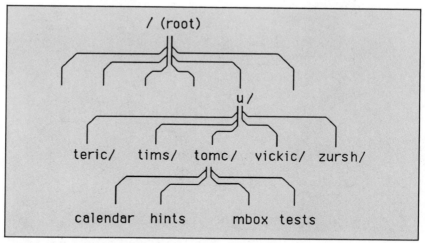

Figure 4.4: *A partial file system tree of the /u directory*

5. Use cd *to go back to your home directory.*

Whenever you want to go "home" from anyplace in the UNIX file system, you can use **cd** without any arguments. This sends you straight back to your own directory again.

6. Use cd pathname *to change to a specific directory.*

To move to a directory that isn't near at hand, you can use **cd** with an argument that specifies the pathname of the directory you want to move to. If you want to change to the root directory, for instance, just enter **cd /**. Then enter **lf** to list the files and directories in that directory. You'll probably see a mixture of files and directories that looks something like this:

bin/	**dev/**	**install/**	**tmp/**	**usr/**
boot	**dos**	**lib/**	**u/**	**wastebasket/**
clipdir/	**etc/**	**lost + found/**		**unix**

You know already that all of the users on the whole system are in the **/u** directory. Small names don't mean small directories; in fact, if you want to make a general rule, the most important things in the UNIX file system often have short names (this is because Dennis Ritchie, who made up many of the names, hated to type).

Take a look around while you're here. Figure 4.5 shows the tree with some of the most important directories filled in.

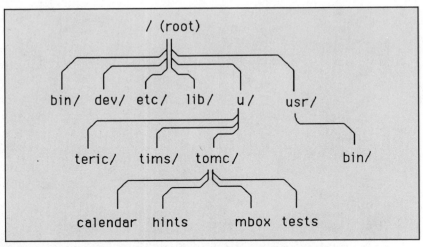

Figure 4.5: *A partial file system tree of the / (root) directory*

7. Look in two different bin directories for the calendar program.

Try to find the calendar program, which looks at the calendar file you wrote in your home directory and sends you reminders on the appropriate dates. It's in a file called calendar*. On most systems, it's either in the /bin or /usr/bin directory, where compiled programs (called *bin*aries) are kept. In almost all UNIX file systems there are several /bin directories scattered in various places around the tree. How can there be more than one /bin directory? Each /bin directory is inside a different directory, so each has a unique *pathname*. As far as UNIX is concerned, files or directories with different paths are different. The pathname of a file, in a sense, is a part of the file's name. If you remember which things are in /bin and which are in /usr/bin you'll do fine.

Any time you are in a directory that has other directories inside it, you can use the command **cd *directoryname*** to change to them. In terms of the directory tree, you use this command to move to any directory that branches down from your working directory.

Enter **cd bin** to move from the root directory to the bin directory inside it. Use **lf** to look for the calendar* file in the /bin directory. The asterisk that appears after files in the /bin directory when you use **lf** tells you that these are *executable* files: programs you start by entering their names as commands. You may not see the calendar* file, but if you look through the listing carefully, you'll see some program files you've used often, like vi* and lf* (which you just used to see the listing). If the listing is so long that part of it scrolls up out of view, see the next step for help.

If you don't see the calendar* file in /bin, you can use another form of the **cd** command to move to the bin directory that is in the /usr directory. This is not a move directly down the directory tree; it is a move across and down, to a different branch or *subdirectory* of the root directory. Look at Figure 4.5 again and you'll see that this move from /bin to /usr/bin is going to take you all the way across the top of the directory tree, and then down a level, under /usr.

Enter **cd /usr/bin** to move from the /bin directory to the /usr/bin directory. This is a **cd** *pathname* command; it tells UNIX exactly where you want to go, giving the full or *absolute* pathname from the root directory down the tree through the usr directory to the bin directory inside it. If you enter the **pwd** command when you get there, you'll see the same path you just used in your **cd** command, /usr/bin.

8. Pipe file listings through more.

Use the **lf** command to list the directories and files in the /usr/bin directory, and find the calendar* file in the listing. If your system is like mine, you'll see many files in this directory—probably too many to be seen at one time on the screen.

Sometimes UNIX tries to show you too much at once. If a file listing (or the output of almost any other command) scrolls off the top of the screen before you can read it, wait until it stops. If it just keeps on whizzing by, press the Delete key to stop it. When the prompt has returned, you can use the **more** command and a *pipe* (| or ¦) to look through the output one screen at a time. A pipe lets you give two commands to the shell in sequence. The output of the first command is "piped" to the second one, which takes that output, works on it, and then gives you a final result. What you finally see is the product of both commands working together, one after the other. Figure 4.6 shows this process.

For instance, enter **lf | more** and press the Return key. (On some terminals, ¦ is used as a pipe character; use whichever one your terminal has.) This tells UNIX to pipe the output of **lf** through the **more** command.

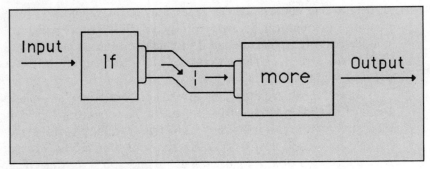

Figure 4.6: *What a pipe does*

When you press Return, the first screenful of the file listing shows on the screen. A prompt appears in reverse video at the bottom of the screen, telling you that there is more to see. Press the spacebar to see another screenful of data, or press Return to see the data a line at a time.

9. Use **more** to look at the contents of a file.

You can use the **more** command to look at what's inside a file, as well what's inside a directory. This can sometimes be helpful if you want to find out what an executable file does. To see the actual program code of the calendar* file, for instance, enter **more calendar** while you are still in the /usr/directory. You don't have to type the star at the end of the file name.

The contents of the file will appear. As before, if you want to look through the calendar program one screen at a time, press the spacebar; to see the file one line at a time, press Return. Most of the code you see here will probably be unintelligible to non-programmers, but the comment lines—the ones that have a # at the left margin—will give you some idea of what the calendar program is and what it does.

10. Move to another directory with relative path commands.

When you used the **cd /usr/bin** command, you moved to that directory very precisely, using an absolute path. This is the best and quickest way to move to directories that are far away from you on the directory tree. If you want to move to a closer directory, however, you can use *relative* commands, which get you someplace in relation to your present directory.

Enter **cd ..** to move from the /usr/bin directory up one level to the /usr directory. (You used this command before to move from your home directory to /u.)

From the /usr directory, enter **cd ../bin** to move across the directory tree to the /bin directory. This tells UNIX to move to the directory above the present one, then move across and down into another directory. Figure 4.7 shows this movement on a file system tree.

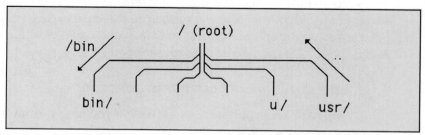

Figure 4.7: *Moving from one directory to another across the directory tree*

If you want some more practice moving across the directory tree, and want to see what's in the other directories within the root, use the relative path commands **cd ../dev** and **cd ../etc** to move from /bin to /dev and /etc. List the files in one or both of these directories, if you want to get a hint of how much there is to learn about the UNIX file system. You can use similar commands to explore any other directories in your root directory.

11. Return to your home directory with a relative path command.

Just to get a little exercise in relative pathnames, use **cd** to return to your home directory, like this:

cd ../u/loginname

Notice that in this case, you move up one level from the directory you are in, then down two levels.

Of course, you could get to the same place by using **cd** by itself, without arguments. When you have had more practice moving around the file system, you will gradually come to use the shortest possible command for any given move. Until then, just use the first command that comes to mind that gets you where you want to go. It's a good idea to practice using them all when you're new to the game; then you'll have more options to draw on as you gain expertise.

Organizing Your Own Files and Directories

Now that you have taken a look around the UNIX file system, you can begin to organize things in your home directory. If you maintain the same clear hierarchy or tree structure that you have seen in the overall file system, you will be able to store lots of data in different files within your home directory, and still remember where they all are.

1. List the contents of your home directory.

Use **lf** to refresh your memory as to what you have in your home directory. I see this:

calendar   mbox   tests   hints

You could just leave those files there, and add more and more files to your home directory until the listing fills up three or four screens. Then any time you wanted to find a file, you would have to look through the whole list for it. That gets time-consuming; it also puts a burden on the operating system.

So for your own sake, and for the sake of speed and efficiency on your UNIX system, limit the files and directories in your home directory. If you can keep the total down to about ten, that's ideal.

2. Use lf -a to see "hidden" files.

There are files in your home directory that you don't normally see. These are files that take care of things behind the scenes. The files all begin with a dot or period (.) and they do not appear in file listings unless you use the **-a** option of the listing command. Enter **lf -a** and you will see the hidden or dot files in your home directory. There will be at least one, namely your .profile file. This is the file that sets things up for you when you log in. There may be other dot files, such as .exrc or .mailrc, or some other file with *rc* at the end. You'll learn about some of them in later chapters of this book. If you are using the C shell (if your system prompt is a **%** instead of a **$**) you will have a .login file and a .cshrc file instead of a .profile file.

3. Use mkdir *to create new directories.*

If you have several mail files in your home directory, make a /News directory by entering **mkdir News** at the system prompt. If you list the contents of the directory with **lf** again, you'll see / News listed along with the files.

Why name the mail directory "News"? If you have an electronic news billboard set up for your system, such as ReadNews, it is likely that it will look for a /News directory in your home directory for any news articles you save off the billboard. If you make the /News directory yourself, you can use it as a convenient place to save both mail messages and future news articles.

Notice that I used an uppercase *N* for the name of the directory. Capitalizing the names of the directories in my home directory makes it that much easier to distinguish them from plain files. In this particular case, our news program puts articles in the /News directory automatically, so that's the way I have to spell it. Of course, you don't have to capitalize your directory names; lots of them in the file system aren't.

Create other directories for groups of files you accumulate. I have to write a lot of outlines in my job, so I should use **mkdir Outlines** to create an /Outlines directory in my home directory. My personal branch of the file system now looks like Figure 4.8.

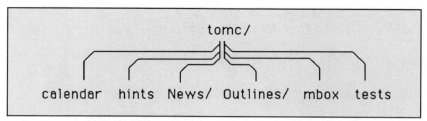

Figure 4.8: *A home directory, with two directories and four files*

Perhaps you create lots of database reports in your job; if you do, you'll want to have a /Reports directory, with several subdirectories inside it for reports on different subjects. You might want to set up subdirectories for the reports for each month, for instance. You can set up your directories and subdirectories in whatever way you want. Remember, though, that everything works better if you only have a few directories in your home directory.

4. Move files into a directory you have created with mv.

To move files from one directory to another, use the **mv *filename directoryname*** command. This command takes two arguments: the file you want to move, and where you want to move it. You can list any number of files to move, as long as the last name in the command is the name of the directory where you want the files to go. For example, if I enter

    mv hints tests News

both of my mail message files go into the /News directory.

It's important to note that it can make for trouble if you forget to put the directory name on the end. For example, if I left off the /News directory in the command above, **mv** would have erased the tests file and renamed the hints file as tests. The contents of the real tests file would be *gone*. (Weird, isn't it?) If you want to use this to your advantage, of course, you could rename a file by using the form **mv *filename newfilename***. Just be careful to pick a new name that does not exist already.

Don't move the calendar and mbox files into any directory other than your home one: since UNIX uses them daily, they have to stay put where UNIX can find them.

5. Combine two commands to move to the /News directory and list its files.

From your home directory you can move down into the News directory and list the files by putting **cd** and **lf** together, like this:

    cd News; lf

Just use a semi-colon (;) and a space between commands, and you can string as many as you want together. When you list the files in your News directory, you ought to see the ones you moved in there. I see my hints and tests files.

6. *Make subdirectories within your directories.*

While I'm in a tidying-up mood, I want to go to my /Outlines directory and arrange it a little. If I want to make directories to separate the outlines for this book from another one, I can go to the Outline directory and subdirectories like this:

cd ../Outlines; mkdir ABCS; mkdir Tutorial

My directory tree now looks like the one in Figure 4.9.

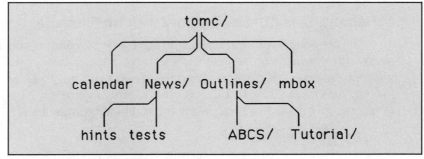

Figure 4.9: *A small directory tree in a home directory*

7. *Copy files from one directory to another with* cp.

As we saw in step 4 above, you can use **mv** in a sort of sneaky way to rename a file, by "moving" it onto itself with a new name. To copy a file without affecting the original at all, use the **cp** command. Move back to the /News directory by typing

cd ../News

Then copy two files from this directory to one of the new ones you created.

In my case, I can copy the files tests and hints into the Tutorial directory under my Outlines directory. If I am in /News, I can give the following commands to copy the files:

cp tests /u/tomc/Outlines/Tutorial/tests
cp hints ../Outlines/Tutorial/hints

Notice that either the absolute path used in the top command or the relative path below it will copy a file into the Tutorial directory. The difference between **cp** and **mv** is that **cp** leaves one copy of the file where it was, and puts a second copy in the new location you specify.

Like **mv**, you can specify more than one filename in a **cp** command, as long as the last thing in the command is a directory name. For instance, I could enter

cp hints tests ../Outlines/Tutorial

to copy two files to the /Tutorial directory at once. This is the kind of shortcut command that can take the boredom out of organizing a number of files.

8. Remove files from a directory with rm filename.

If you decide you don't want or need a file anymore, you can remove it by entering **rm filename** when you are in the directory with the file. For example, I don't really need those two mail files I just copied into my tutorial outlines, so I'll delete them. First, I go to my /Tutorial directory and list the files there, using the combined command

cd ../Outline/Tutorial; lf

Once I'm there, I could delete the files one at a time like this:

rm hints
rm tests

But there's an easier way, using a *wildcard* character, the * (an asterisk, star, or splat, depending on who you talk to). This is a single character that can stand for all characters in a file or directory name, like a wildcard in a poker game. If you want a command to act on several files that have the same letters or numbers in them, you can specify those letters, and use the wildcard character to take care of the rest.

Obviously, you have to be careful with the wildcard character: it's very easy to delete something by mistake. Make sure you leave enough characters specified to limit your deletion, and *never* use **rm ***, without any other characters specified. This will remove every file in the working directory.

So here I am in my /Tutorial directory. Both of the files I want to remove end in **s**, and there are no files which end in **s** that I must save. So I can enter

rm *s

to delete both the hints and the tests files in one quick command.

What about the hints and tests files in the /News directory? I don't have to worry about the command removing them, because **rm *s** only takes effect on files in the current working directory. Move to the /News directory and list the files if you want to check it out.

9. Use the rmdir directoryname command to remove an unwanted directory.

If you make a mistake in the spelling of a directory name, or if you decide you don't need a directory, you can remove it, but only if there are no files or directories in it. For instance, if I created a directory in my Outlines directory named "Futorial" instead of "Tutorial," I could remove the misspelled directory by typing

rmdir Futorial

as long as I had not yet put anything inside it. If you try to remove a directory with files in it, UNIX tells you the directory is not empty. You must remove the files or move them to other directories before you remove the directory.

Working with Permissions

1. Use lf -l to see the permissions on your files.

In order to see file permissions, you need to add an argument to the usual **lf** command. Enter

lf -l

to list a *l*ong version of a directory list. In my sample home directory, the long list looks like this:

```
total 4
drwxrwxr-x   2 tomc pub 80 Jun 23 14:06 News/
drwxrwxr-x   4 tomc pub 64 Jun 23 13:10 Outlines/
-rw-rw-r--   1 tomc pub 435 Apr 14 10:16 calendar
-rw-rw-r--   1 tomc pub 118 Jun 16 16:43 mbox
```

The first line of the listing tells the total number of blocks of memory (each block is 1024 bytes) the directory takes up on the hard disk.

The permissions are shown in the series of letters on the left of the file names; you will notice that there are ten characters in each permissions line. A sample permissions line for a typical file is shown in Figure 4.10.

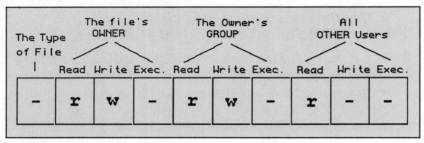

Figure 4.10: *A typical permissions line*

As you can see, each position within the line has its own particular meaning. The first character is either d for directory or - (a hyphen) for a plain file. (There are other abbreviations for special types of files, but we won't go into them here.) In the listing from the lf -l command, you'll notice that the two d-flagged directories are listed first: /News and /Outlines.

The next nine permissions are always listed in the order shown, although the permissions actually granted will vary from file to file. The meaning of the different letters is as follows:

r   read

w   write

x   execute

-       permission not granted

This may sound a little confusing at first, but it gets easy pretty quickly. Just to simplify things a little, let's look at the permissions for one file at a time. You will want to do this as a general rule, anyway; often a lf -l list will be too long to search through if you're looking for information about one file.

2. Use l filename *to display the permissions for a single file.*

Do a long listing for one file by just typing l (an "el"), a space, and the file name. For instance, when I enter

l calendar

I see the following:

-rw-rw-r-- 1 tomc pub 435 Apr 14 10:16 calendar

This is the same thing you saw in the previous example, but for one file, instead of for all the files in your directory. Let's look a little closer at this information: UNIX packs a lot into that single line. As you read from left to right, you can tell the file's

- Type: from the first character of that ten-character code, either **d**, for directory,- for file, **b**, **c**, or **p** for special files.
- Permissions: who can read, write, and execute the file.
- Links: connections to other files in the file system.
- Owner: the user who created the file.
- Group: the workgroup that the owner of the file shares data with.
- Size: the number of bytes of memory the file requires.
- Date and Time: the last time the file was modified.
- Name: the name the owner gave the file.

As the user who created the calendar file, I can read it and write to it but not execute it. People in my group can also read it and write to it but not execute it. All the other users on the system can read the file but they can neither write to it nor execute it. The permissions for your calendar file might be a bit different, but they should be similar.

3. Change file permissions with chmod.

To keep other people from reading my calendar file, all I have to do is take away their read permissions. I enter

chmod go-r calendar

In the command, the **g** stands for group and the **o** stands for others. The characters **-r** take away read permission. If I want to make sure nobody in my group writes any bogus dates in my calendar, I can use the command

chmod g-w calendar

to prevent that. If I enter **l calendar** now, I see the following:

-rw------- 1 tomc pub 435 April 14 10:16 calendar

Ignoring that first "I am a file" dash, the next nine characters tell you that I still have read and write permissions to it, but nobody else has any permissions at all.

If you are on a small UNIX system and you can trust the other users, you could enter

chmod a + w calendar

to give everybody write permission for your calendar file. The **a** in this command stands for all users. Use the **l** calendar command to see the write permissions that all of the categories of users now have. The good thing about giving permissions like these is that they let other people change things if they need to. For example, if you are sick and can't come in to work, you can have a co-worker change your calendar to cancel appointment reminders or set new ones.

One cautionary note about permissions: don't change the permissions for directories without studying an advanced text on UNIX. The permissions on directories look just like those for files, but what they do is more complex and much more far-reaching in effect.

Finding a Particular File in the System

If you can't remember where a file is in your directory tree, you can use the **find** command to do the searching for you.

1. Get into the most likely directory.

Limit your search if you can by moving to the closest directory you think might have the file. For instance, if you know the file you're looking for is somewhere inside your home directory, **cd** there. If you know the file is in one of several directories, go to the directory one level above them. The important thing is to limit the size of your eventual search as much as you can. For instance, don't invoke **find** from the root directory unless you absolutely can't find a file in any other way; you'll find that searching through the whole file system is hard—and time-consuming—work, for the computer.

2. Use find . -name filename -print *to find the file.*

If I want to look for my hints file, starting from my home directory, I can use the **find** command like this:

cd; find . -name hints -print

When you use **find,** make sure you put a space, the period, and another space for the first argument after the find command, so it will start looking for the named file in your working directory, and go down from there. It makes a very thorough search, through every directory in your tree, and tells you all of the files you have with the name specified.

A word to the wise: if you find yourself using the find command often in your own home directory, you probably need to reorganize your files and directories. Keep in mind that if you have too many files and directories in any one directory, you slow down the whole UNIX system every time it searches for somebody's missing file.

*T*roubleshooting

I got lost in the file system.

It's a spooky feeling, isn't it? But it can happen to anyone, even experienced UNIX users, so several remedies have been developed. If all you want to know is where you are, just use the **pwd** command to see the absolute path from the root directory to your working one. If you want to go home, right now, so you can get your bearings and eat some of your mom's cooking before you venture out into the UNIX cafe again, just use the **cd** command with no arguments.

I got a permission denied *message when I tried to read or write to a file.*

You don't have the permissions needed. If you don't own the file (if you didn't create it, in other words), contact the owner and have him or her use **chmod** to change the permissions so you can read or write to the file.

You can also get this error message if you try to vi a file without entering **vi** before the file name. It can happen if you forget to enter any file-handling command before you enter the file name. In these cases, you don't have to change any permissions. You just have to wake up and use the commands correctly; command first, file name afterward. And don't forget the space, there, cadet.

I got a cannot make directory *message after entering a command.*

This will happen if you are in a directory where you don't have permission to do things. For instance, if you are in the /etc directory and you try to **mkdir foosplat** you will see an error message like:

mkdir: cannot make directory "foosplat".

You do not have permission to create directories. So you'll just have to make your foosplat directory someplace else.

I got a cannot copy file to itself *message when I tried to cp a file.*

If you try to copy a file to a directory and there is already a file with that name in the directory, you will get this error. Change the filename beforehand, if necessary, using the **mv** *filename newfilename* command.

*C*ommand Summary

COMMAND	DESCRIPTION
cd *directoryname*	Changes to named directory that is inside working directory.

COMMAND	DESCRIPTION
cd *pathname*	Changes directory; pathname can be absolute (from root down), or relative (from working directory).
chmod u,g,o,a ± rwx *filename*	Changes permissions of *u*ser, *g*roup, *o*thers, or *a*ll users; add (+) or remove (−) *r*ead, *w*rite, *e*xecute permission for named file.
l *filename*	Displays long listing of information about named file. Can be used to list contents of directories, too.
lf	Lists files in working directory.
lf -a	Lists all files in working directory, including hidden.
lf -l	Displays long listing of information about files in working directory.
mkdir *directoryname*	Makes a directory with the specified name.
more *filename*	Displays contents of a file one screen at a time. Use also with a pipe (	) for extensive listings.
rm *filename*	Removes file with specified name.
rmdir *directoryname*	Removes directory with specified name; all files in the directory must first be removed.
| more	Pipes output through more command. Preceded by l or lf commands to display extensive file listings one screen at a time.

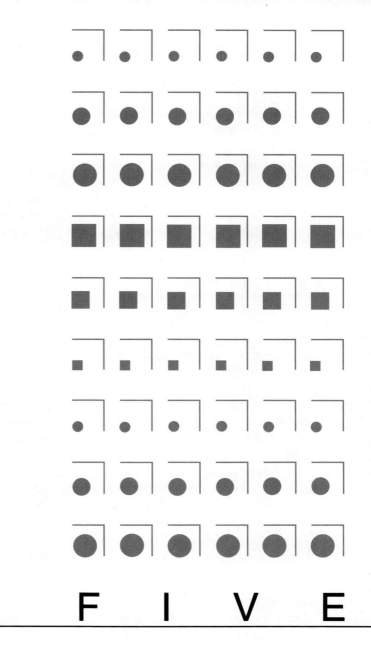

F I V E

**Saving Copies
of Your Files**

This chapter explains how to save copies of files that are important to your work. If something happens to an original file, you can use the backup copy and continue working. Some applications give you easy ways to save backup copies of files as you work, but some don't, and you may want to save your work in a way that the application does not provide for. This chapter describes the procedures for saving files in a number of places; in your working directory, in another directory on the file system, on a floppy disk, and on a tape.

Making a Backup Copy of a File

Use the following procedure to make a copy of any file you want to protect while you work on it. Sometimes it can make a great deal of difference in your work if you have a backup copy of a file, even if you aren't making major changes to the file.

For example, if you have created a detailed spreadsheet that shows the company is doing well this quarter, but you have to make some last-minute changes before presenting the spreadsheet at a meeting, make a copy of the spreadsheet file before you do your final edit. That way, if you make a mistake while editing the file and your mistake skews the balance deep into the red, you can use the backup file to make your presentation at the meeting.

The following procedure explains how make a convenient copy of any standard file, no matter what application was used to create the file.

1. List the files in your working directory.

You need to see the names of all files in the working directory so you can make sure you are copying the file with the correct name, and also to make sure you don't make a backup filename that overwrites another file in the directory. If I use the **lf** command in my /u/tomc/ Outlines/Tutorial directory, for instance, I see the following files:

    chapt1   chapt2   chapt3   chapt4

I can now look at the name of the file I want to back up to make sure I spell it correctly. Since there aren't any backup files there already, I don't have to worry about overwriting anything.

2. Make a backup copy of your file.

Use the **cp** *filename* command. It's best to give the backup file the same name as the original file, and add a period and the letters **bk** or **bak** so you recognize it immediately.

For instance, if I want to make a backup of my chapt1 outline, I can enter

cp chapt1 chapt1.bak

to make an easily recognized backup. If I list the files again, I see this:

chapt1   chapt1.bak   chapt2   chapt3   chapt4

Now I don't have to worry about the possibility of losing or scrambling chapt1 as I work on it.

3. After major modifications, make a new backup.

If you want a backup file to remain useful, you have to update it after changing the original. You can use the same name for the new backup copy as you did for the old one; the **cp** command just overwrites the old backup copy. In my example, I could just enter

cp chapt1 chapt1.bak

again, and the new chapt1.bak would replace the old one. You may be asked by a prompt if you want to overwrite the old file, depending on how your system works.

Copying Finished Files to a Separate Directory

When you finish work on a project, you should make backups of all the files and keep these backups in a different directory from the one you normally work in. This protects the files from accidental overwrites and mistaken modifications. You can change the permissions for the backup files to further protect them.

1. Make a directory to store the backup files.

You can keep groups of backup files in directories that are "shadows" of the directories with the original files. Make a hierarchy with the same subdirectory names, but with a different directory at the top. For instance, if I want to back up files in the Outlines directory in my home directory, I can make an Outlinesbk directory in my home directory. Inside the Outlinesbk directory I can make ABCS and Tutorial directories, so the backup files can be put in the same hierarchy as the original files. In terms of my directory tree, it looks like Figure 5.1. The backups will go in directories with the same names as the originals, so they'll be easy to find.

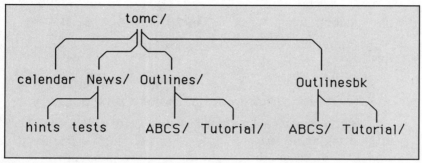

Figure 5.1: *Shadow directories for backups*

2. Make backup copies of your files in a separate directory.

You can copy files into your new backup directory with the **cp** command in the form

cp *filename directoryname*

If I am in my /u/tomc/Outlines/Tutorial directory, for example, I can send chapt1.bak to my "shadow" backup directory as follows:

cp chapt1.bak /u/tomc/Outlinesbk/Tutorial

Since the second argument to **cp** begins with a slash character, UNIX knows that you want to send a copy of the file to another directory, rather than making a copy with that name in the current one.

If I wanted to copy all the files in my directory to the shadow directory, though, this command would be cumbersome to type over and over. Instead, I could use wildcard characters to copy a number of files at the same time.

For instance, if I am in the /u/tomc/Outlines/Tutorial directory, I can send all my Tutorial chapter outline files to the shadow Tutorial directory with the following command:

cp chapt? /u/tomc/Outlinesbk/Tutorial

Note that this wildcard command does not recopy the file chapt1.bak; the **cp chapt?** command copies only those files with six characters, the first five of which are **chapt**. Used as a wildcard, **?** in a file name stands for any single character.

3. Change the permissions of the copied files.

If you want to make sure nobody changes the backup files you have made, you can change the permissions for the files. The command

chmod go-w *filename*

will remove the write permission for all users other than you. To protect my chapt1.bak file, I would enter

chmod go-w chapt1.bak

You can use wildcards in this command also; for example, if I am in the backup directory of my Tutorial chapter outlines, I can enter

chmod go-w chapt?

and all the chapt files will be safe from modification by any users other than me. Again, the **?** wildcard character stands for any single character, so this command will protect only files beginning with **chapt** and having one more character at the end. (For more information about permissions, see Chapter 4.)

4. Take care when you put a backup copy back.

It's safest to make copying backups a one-way street *from* the original *to* the backup directory. Otherwise, you can overwrite a later version of a file with an outdated backup copy. For instance, if I made changes to my chapt1 file in the original directory, I would lose those modifications if I copied the chapt1 backup directory file back into the original directory.

Saving Files to a Disk: Archiving

If you have finished work on a major project and want to make a permanent copy of a whole directory containing all your critical files, the safest way is to put the directory on a floppy disk and keep this floppy disk in a secure place. The formal name for this process is *archiving:* you are making a personal library, or *archive,* of your finished work. To do this, you need to get a floppy disk that your system's computer can write to, then log in on the computer's console, and copy your directory of the hard disk onto the floppy disk. The UNIX utility that you use to copy the files is **tar,** derived from *t*ape *ar*chive. The process of archiving on floppy disks is informally called *tarring off.*

1. Obtain a disk
and the device number for the disk drive.

Contact your system administrator or a fellow user who has done a lot of archiving on floppy disks. Find out where the appropriate floppy disks are and get one. Then find out what the device number is for the floppy-disk drive that you are going to put the disk into. On most systems, there will be a one-digit *key* number for the floppy-disk drive. You also need to know the full device number, which will be much longer. Two examples on my UNIX system are device numbers rfd096ds15 and rfd0135ds18; they have the key numbers 2 and 6 respectively. They refer to a floppy-disk drive for 5^1/$_4$-inch, 1.2Mb floppy-disks and one for 3^1/$_2$-inch, 1.5Mb floppy disks.

If you have a hints file in your News directory, it might be good to e-mail yourself a letter with the device and key numbers, with a subject like "Floppy device number" so you can find it easily for future reference.

2. Log in on the console of your system's computer.

The console is a special keyboard and monitor you will use to interact with the computer. Check with the system administrator to make sure nobody needs to use the console for the next half hour, then log in just as you would on your own terminal. If you are prompted for a terminal type, check with your system administrator. The console is often set up to operate as an *ansi* terminal. If it is, enter **ansi** for the terminal type.

When you see the system prompt, you are ready to format your floppy disk and tar files onto it.

3. Insert the floppy disk and format it.

If you can get them, use new, error-free floppy disks at all times. If you are using either a new floppy disk or an old one that needs to be reformatted, enter the following command at the console:

format /dev/*devicenumber*

For example, if I want to format a 5¼-inch, 1.2Mb floppy disk, I enter

format /dev/rfd096ds15

and press Return. When you enter the format command, use your own device number, of course. After you press the Return key, UNIX responds with the following message:

insert floppy in drive; press <RETURN> when ready

Turn the disk drive handle out of the way, slide the floppy disk into the floppy disk drive, and press the Return key. UNIX will proceed to format the floppy disk. It will tell you how many tracks it has formatted and verified, and tells you when formatting and verifying are done.

4. Change to the directory with the files you want to copy.

Type **cd *pathname*; lf** to change to the directory you need to be in and list its files. For example, if I want to tar off all my chapter outlines for my Tutorial, I enter the following command:

The result appears:

```
chapt1       chapt2       chapt3       chapt4
chapt1.bak   chapt2.bak   chapt3.bak   chapt4.bak
```

I could just make copies of each of these files onto the floppy disk; if this is all you need to do, go on to step 6. You may need to organize the files into subdirectories, however, and copy the whole hierarchy onto the floppy disk.

5. Organize your files if necessary.

If you are tarring files with the same names onto a floppy disk, make sure you keep them in separate directories or some of them will get overwritten. For instance, if I want to tar off my chapt1 and chapt2 outlines for my ABCS book at the same time I tar off the Tutorial chapter files, I cannot copy them into the Tutorial outline directory, or they will overwrite the first and second chapter outlines of the Tutorial. To solve this problem I can make a temporary subdirectory in the Tutorial directory with a name like "ABCStmp" and copy the chapt1 and chapt2 files from the ABCS book into it. The **tar** utility will copy the whole hierarchy in Figure 5.2 onto the floppy disk.

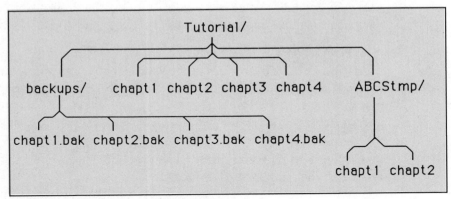

Figure 5.2: *A temporary directory for tarring off*

If some of the files you want to copy could be in a subdirectory, and you want to copy all of them onto the floppy disk, make a subdirectory and use the **mv** command to put them there. For more information on this procedure, see Chapter 4, "Learning About Files and Directories."

Check the main directory and each subdirectory with the **lf** command. Everything the way you planned? Good.

6. Check the size of the directory you want to copy.

You need to make sure that you have enough room on your floppy disk for the directory you want to copy. If you are in the directory you want to tar off, enter

du -a

This reports the *d*isk *u*sage needed for *a*ll of the files in the working directory. If I enter **du -a** while I'm in my Tutorial directory, I get the following report:

```
 44   ./ABCStmp/chapt1
 66   ./ABCStmp/chapt2
112   ./ABCStmp/
 52   ./chapt1
 70   ./chapt2
 36   ./chapt3
128   ./chapt4
 50   ./backups/chapt1.bak
 68   ./backups/chapt2.bak
 36   ./backups/chapt3.bak
128   ./backups/chapt4.bak
304   ./backups
704
```

The crucial number in this report is the one at the bottom. It tells how many half-kilobyte blocks of storage the working directory and all its contents take up. To get a quick idea of how many kilobytes of space the directory needs on the floppy disk, all you have to do is divide that number in half. In the sample shown, the directory would take up about 352K (or .352Mb, since there are a thousand kilobytes in every megabyte) of space on the floppy disk. So it would fit on a 1.2Mb or a 1.5Mb floppy disk easily. If your directory is too big for one floppy disk, the easiest thing to do is move some of the files into a different directory, then copy each directory to a different floppy disk.

You can also format several floppy disks, and let tar divide the archive among them automatically. The problem with this approach is that the files are not divided logically between the different floppy disks, so you may have trouble finding files later on.

7. *Use* tar cvkeynumber .
to copy the directory onto the floppy disk.

When everything is set up the way you want it, and you are sure it is not too big to fit on the floppy disk, enter the tar command:

tar *cvkeynumber* .

Notice that the tar command does not use options with a dash or minus sign in front of them. Instead, it uses a key letter, then any options you want, and then a key number. The key letter in the command above is **c** to *c*reate a backup directory, or archive. The letter **v** is the verbose option; it indicates that UNIX will report back to you every time it copies a file to the floppy disk. If there is no one-digit key number for the floppy-disk drive on your system's computer, you have to enter the full device number, using the

tar **cvf** *devicename* .

form of the tar command. The **f** stands for file, and it means "use the device file named in the next argument."

Whichever form of the command you use, make sure you include the period at the end before you press Return. It stands for the current or working directory (another example of Dennis Ritchie's penchant for giving important things short names).

On my local machine, all I have to enter is

tar **cv2** .

and the floppy-disk drive begins to whirr. If I didn't have that handy key number, I would have to enter

tar **cvf /dev/rfd096ds15** .

to copy my directory to the floppy disk.

If you have entered the command correctly, and if the archiving process works as it should, you will soon see a report of what was written on the floppy disk. In my case, it looks like this:

```
Volume ends at 1199K, blocking factor = 5K

Seek = 23K     a    ./ABCStmp/chapt1 23K
Seek = 58K     a.   /ABCStmp/chapt2 35K
Seek = 86K     a    ./chapt1 28K
Seek = 122K    a    ./chapt2 36K
Seek = 142K    a    ./chapt3 20K
```

```
Seek = 208K   a   ./chapt4 66K
Seek = 235K   a   ./backups/chapt1.bak 27K
Seek = 271K   a   ./backups/chapt2.bak 36K
Seek = 291K   a   ./backups/chapt3.bak 20K
Seek = 357K   a   ./backups/chapt4.bak 66K
```

In the first line of information, **Volume** means the floppy disk. My floppy disk holds 1199K, or just under 1.2Mb. **Blocking factor** means that data is being copied in 5K units. As copying proceeds, **tar** reports how much room it is seeking for the files, and how much space each file takes up. The total space sought builds up until the last file is copied. Then your system prompt returns.

8. List the files on the floppy disk.

If you want to check the contents of the floppy disk to make sure you copied all the files you wanted, use **tar tv***keynumber* (this command doesn't take a period). The **t** stands for *t*able of contents. If you don't have a keynumber, use the long device number, as explained in the last step. If I can use the keynumber 2 to designate my floppy-disk drive, I can enter **tar tv2** to see the listing shown in Figure 5.3.

```
-rw-rw-r--4734/104   23106  Jul  10  15:55  1991  ./ABCStmp/chapt1
-rw-rw-r--4734/104   35721  Jul  10  15:55  1991  ./ABCStmp/chapt2
-rw-rw-r--4734/104   28439  Jul  09  18:34  1991  ./chapt1
-rw-rw-r--4734/104   36063  Jul  09  13:47  1991  ./chapt2
-rw-rw-r--4734/104   20643  Jul  09  13:47  1991  ./chapt3
-rw-rw-r--4734/104   66290  Jul  09  13:48  1991  ./chapt4
-rw-rw-r--4734/104   27502  Jul  10  18:34  1991  ./backups/chapt1.bak
-rw-rw-r--4734/104   36029  Jul  10  13:45  1991  ./backups/chapt2.bak
-rw-rw-r--4734/104   20115  Jul  10  13:45  1991  ./backups/chapt3.bak
-rw-rw-r--4734/104   66287  Jul  10  13:46  1991  ./backups/chapt4.bak
```

Figure 5.3: *Files and directories archived on a floppy disk*

You can use a listing like this one to check not only filenames, but the sizes of the files and their permissions. The sizes are listed to the left of the dates, and the permissions are listed at the left end of the lines. Everything should be the same as it was in the directory you copied the files from.

102   *The ABC's of SCO UNIX*

CH. 5

9. Clean up and log out of the console.

If you made directories to separate files with the same names, remove the files from those directories with the **rm** command and remove the directories with the **rmdir** command. For example, I would enter

cd ABCStmp; rm ch*

to go to my ABCStmp directory and remove the files there. Then I would enter

cd ..; rmdir ABCStmp

to go up one level and delete the ABCStmp directory, so my Tutorial directory would only have outlines from my tutorial in it.

After housecleaning, log out of your system's computer console. This is just like logging out of your own terminal; use either **exit** or **Ctrl-d**, whichever you usually would.

10. Store your floppy disk properly.

Don't take any chances on losing the floppy disk with your backup files. If there is no label on the floppy disk, make one. Put the floppy in a protective sleeve as soon as you have labeled it.

Store the disk in a place where it will be kept cool, dry, and dust-free, and where it will not be exposed to anything magnetic. If you have to store numerous floppy disks, obtain a disk box or file, and organize them by date, by subject, or both. Nothing is as useless as a large, disordered collection of floppy disks—especially when you need a backup copy of a file in a hurry.

Adding to an Archive on a Disk

If you create one or two additional files for a project after archiving a directory to a floppy disk, you can add the new files to the end of the existing archive.

On some systems, you may have problems adding to existing floppy-disk archives. See your system administrator to make sure your system has the latest operating system software. If you still have trouble adding to an archive, you may need to put the new files on separate floppy disks.

After major revisions, it is best to archive a whole directory rather than lots of individual files. Not only is it less time-consuming, it makes for a less confusing archive. The only question is whether you should create a new archive, or overwrite the old one with the new one.

If you don't have enough floppy disks, and if you are sure all the new files are improvements of the old ones, then you can write the new versions of the files over the previously backed-up versions on the floppy disk.

If you have plenty of empty floppy disks, it is better to save the old archive and create a whole new one. Just follow the steps previously discussed in this chapter for saving files to a floppy disk.

1. Log in on the console of your system's computer.

This step is the same as the first step in the standard archiving procedure. Log in as you would at your own terminal, entering **ansi** for the terminal type, if that is what your console is. When you see the system prompt, use **cd** to go to the directory containing the new files you want to tar off.

2. Move all the new files to the same directory.

If you have more than one file to add to the archive, put them in the same directory so you can tar them off all at once. For instance, if I add a chapter 5 outline to my outline files in the Tutorial directory, and also add a chapt5.bak file to the Tutorial/backups directory, I will want to archive both the original file and the backup, to be consistent with the rest of the archive. To prepare for this, I can **cd** to the backups directory and enter **cp chapt5.bak ..** to put a copy of the backup file with chapt5 in the Tutorial directory. If I list the files in the Tutorial directory now, this is what I see:

```
ABCSt     chapt1    chapt3    chapt5
backups   chapt2    chapt4    chapt5.bak
```

The new files, chapt5 and chapt5.bak, are together and ready for tarring off.

3. Check the size of the directory you want to copy.

If you think the addition of your new files may overfill the floppy disk, enter **du -a** when you are in the directory with your new files. Divide the number of blocks for each file in half and add one to see how many kilobytes you are going to add to the floppy disk. In my case, I know I have plenty of room left on the floppy disk, so I can skip this step.

4. Insert the archive disk into the drive and list its contents.

Put the floppy disk in the disk drive and enter **tar tvkey*number*** to list the files on the disk. If I insert the floppy disk I used in the previous archiving procedure, I see the listing shown back in Figure 5.3 again.

Notice that the backup chapter outline files for the Tutorial in this archive are in a backups subdirectory.

5. Add files to the archive on the floppy disk.

To do this, enter

tar rvkey*number* filename

The key letter **r** in the **tar rv** command stands for write (believe it or not). When you invoke **tar** with **r**, it puts the files you list at the end of the archive that already exists on the floppy disk. For example, if I enter the command

tar rv2 chapt5 chapt5.bak

when I'm in the Tutorial directory, I see the following message:

```
Volume ends at 1199K, blocking factor = 5K
Seek = 33K   a    chapt5 33K
Seek = 66K   a    chapt5.bak 33K
```

The whirring disk drive and the message tell me that the files have been written to the disk, but I don't know what has happened to the archive that was already there.

6. List the contents of the floppy disk.

Use the **tar tv***keynumber* command again. This tells you if both the new and the old files are on the floppy disk. If I enter **tar tv2,** I see the table of contents shown in Figure 5.4.

```
-rw-rw-r--4734/104  23106  Jul  10  15:55  1991  ./ABCStmp/chapt1
-rw-rw-r--4734/104  35721  Jul  10  15:55  1991  ./ABCStmp/chapt2
-rw-rw-r--4734/104  28439  Jul  09  18:34  1991  ./chapt1
-rw-rw-r--4734/104  36063  Jul  09  13:47  1991  ./chapt2
-rw-rw-r--4734/104  20643  Jul  09  13:47  1991  ./chapt3
-rw-rw-r--4734/104  66290  Jul  09  13:48  1991  ./chapt4
-rw-rw-r--4734/104  27502  Jul  10  18:34  1991  ./backups/chapt1.bak
-rw-rw-r--4734/104  36029  Jul  10  13:45  1991  ./backups/chapt2.bak
-rw-rw-r--4734/104  20115  Jul  10  13:45  1991  ./backups/chapt3.bak
-rw-rw-r--4734/104  66287  Jul  10  13:46  1991  ./backups/chapt4.bak
-rw-rw-r--4734/104  33472  Jul  12  10:49  1991  chapt5
-rw-rw-r--4734/104  33250  Jul  12  13:07  1991  chapt5.bak
```

Figure 5.4: *New files tarred onto an existing archive disk*

It's all there: the two new files are listed at the bottom, and all the previously archived files are still listed above it.

Notice that the files I archived as part of a directory all have the dot and the slash in front of them, whereas the files I archived by themselves have no dot and slash. This difference is significant when you retrieve the files, so make note of it.

7. Clean up and log out of the console.

Remember to label or relabel any floppy disk to which you have added an archive, and store all of the archive floppy disks properly. Be sure to log out of the console.

Extracting Files from a Floppy-Disk Archive

Backing up files and tarring them off to floppy disks seems like a nuisance until you lose a really important file. Then you'll think archives are great to have around. It goes without saying, therefore, that you should be careful when retrieving a file from a floppy-disk archive.

1. Log in on the console of the system's computer.

Log into the console as before, and put the archive floppy disk into the floppy-disk drive. If you have done a good job labeling your archive disks, you should be able to find the missing files easily.

2. List the floppy disk's files.

To make sure you have the right floppy disk, list its contents as before, with **tar tv** *keynumber*. For example, if I need to extract one of my outline files, I would insert the Tutorial archive disk and enter **tar tv2** to see the list of files shown in Figure 5.4 again.

3. Make a temporary directory for the retrieved file.

In my case, I will enter

mkdir tmp; cd tmp

in my Tutorial directory to first make a new directory and then move into it. My directory tree inside the Tutorial directory now looks like Figure 5.5.

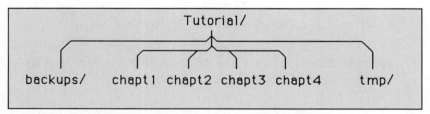

Figure 5.5: *The Tutorial directory with a new tmp directory in it*

This is a precaution against overwriting a file with the same name; never overlook it. For instance, if I lost my chapt5 file and tried to extract it directly into the Tutorial directory, I would run the risk of overwriting other files if I made a simple typing error. If I typed **chapt4** instead of **chapt5** when entering the **tar** command, for instance, UNIX would extract the old chapt4 file and overwrite the current one. Any new work I had done on chapt4 would be lost.

If you already have a tmp directory for some reason, make one with a different name, like tmp.1 or tmp.2, to avoid possible errors. Make absolutely sure you're in the right place with the **pwd** command, and you're ready to go.

4. Extract a file from the floppy disk.

Use the command

tar xvkeynumber filename

The **x** stands for extract. You need to enter the file name exactly as it appears in the listing you got when you entered the **tar tv** command. If there is a dot and a slash in front of the file name in the listing, put them in. If there is nothing in front of the file name, just enter the file name. If the file is in a subdirectory on the archive disk, be sure to enter the whole pathname.

For example, if I have lost my chapt5 outline in my Tutorial directory, I need to extract the chapt5 file from my archive disk. To do this, I type **tar xv2 ./chapt5** and press Return. The tar utility reports the extraction as follows:

x./chapt5, 66290 bytes, 66K

If you have had the great misfortune to lose or delete a whole directory and all of its subdirectories, you can extract a whole directory from a floppy disk by entering **tar xvkeynumber** without arguments. This extracts all of the files from the floppy disk, keeping them in their specified directories. The whole hierarchy appears in your working directory. You may have to move a couple of added files into the right directories after the extraction. For instance, I would have to move the chapt5.bak file into the backups directory, since it was archived separately from the other files.

5. Check the file and move it to its proper place.

Look at the file you extracted with vi, or with whatever application created it. When you are sure it is all there and in its proper form, use the command

mv filename ..

to move the file out of the temporary directory into the directory above, or use

> **mv** *filename pathname*

to move the file to another directory. Just make sure you don't move it to the wrong directory and overwrite a file with the same name.

For example, if I extracted the chapt5 file from the floppy disk, I would enter

> **mv chapt5 ..**

to move it into my Tutorial directory.

When you have moved the file to its proper directory, **cd** to that directory and list the files to make sure the retrieved file is there.

6. Clean up and and log out of the console.

Change back to the directory that contains the tmp directory you made, then use the **rmdir** command to remove any subdirectories and the temporary directory you made for your extracted file. Remove the floppy disk from the disk drive and replace it in its box or file. Log out of the console of the system's computer. You are now ready to go back to your terminal, log in, and go to work, using your extracted file.

Saving Directories in Tape Archives

Backing up your work on a magnetic tape is usually the work of the system administrator. There are many different ways that both complete and partial backups of the system can be done, and these schemes require more explanation than this book can provide.

If your system has a tape drive, and the system administrator is not already taking care of a daily backup of the whole system, you may be able to obtain a tape to back up all your files for a personal archive. You can treat this tape just as you would a floppy disk. The procedures for tarring directories are the same: simply change the key-number or device number to the one for the tape drive on your system. You will not have to format the tape as you have to format a floppy disk, unless you are using a "mini-tape." See your system administrator for instructions on how to insert and remove the tape from the tape drive. After you have begun an archive on a tape, make sure you add all subsequent archives with the **tar rvkeynumber** command, so you don't overwrite an old archive with a new one.

You can extract files from the tape just as you would extract them from a floppy disk, but you may have to do some searching if the file you want is one of many that have been tarred off to the tape. If you use the **tar tvkeynumber** command to list the contents of the tape, pipe the output through the **more** command, so that you can search through a long listing one screenful at a time. For example, if I have archived my whole home directory tree onto a tape device with the keynumber 5, I can enter the following command:

    tar tv5 | more

The files and directories will be listed just as they are in Figure 5.4, but the list will be much longer. You can search for a specific file name if you use **more**; when you have a screenful of listings, enter **/filename** to find the file. For instance, if I wanted to search for chapt1.bak, I could enter **/chapt1.bak** and the listing would scroll down to that file.

Troubleshooting

I get an error message when I try to format a floppy disk.

If the error message says **format:** at the beginning, you may have the wrong type of floppy disk in the disk drive, or the floppy disk may have flaws on it, or you may not have inserted the floppy disk in the disk drive properly.

Try taking the floppy disk out, putting it back in, and turning the handle to the closed position; give the **format** command again. If that doesn't work, see your system administrator or an experienced user, and make sure you are using the right kind of floppy disk. If you have the right type, try another one of the same type, just in case the first one you had was flawed.

After entering the tar cvkeynumber
command, I get a tar: Missing filenames *error message.*

You forgot to put the period at the end of the command, or you forgot to enter any file names. Enter the command again and add the period if you want to tar off the whole working directory and all its subdirectories. Enter the command with file names at the end if you want to tar only one or two files.

After entering the tar tv *or* tar cv
command, I get a tar: tape read *error message.*

The computer is not trying to read a tape, even though that's what it says. It is having trouble reading the floppy disk you inserted.

Either there is no floppy disk in the disk drive, or it is not inserted properly, or the handle is not in the closed position. Take the floppy disk out, put it back in carefully, and turn the handle to the closed position, then try the command again. If the computer still cannot read the floppy disk, it may be damaged. Try inserting it over again several times, and if you have no success, see your system administrator for help.

*C*ommand Summary

COMMAND	DESCRIPTION
du -a	Tells how much disk space current directory needs.
format /dev/*devicenumber*	Formats floppy disk in floppy disk drive with the specified device number.
tar cv*keynumber* .	Copies current directory to floppy disk in disk drive with specified key number.
tar cv*keynumber* *filename*	Copies specified file to floppy disk in disk drive with specified key number.

COMMAND	DESCRIPTION
tar rv*keynumber filename*	Adds specified files to archive on floppy disk in disk drive with specified key number.
tar tv*keynumber*	Displays the table of contents of the floppy disk in disk drive with specified key number.

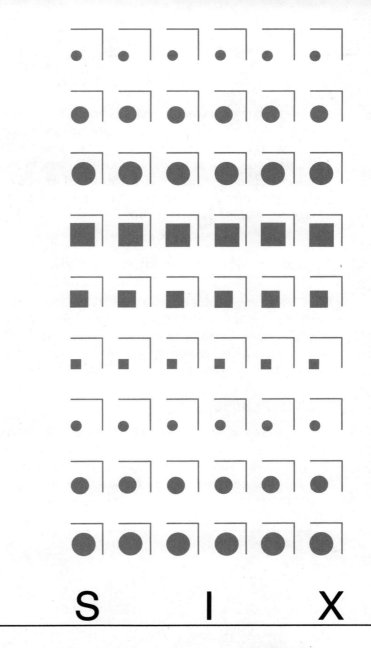

S I X

Printing
with UNIX

Printing can work in a number of different ways on a UNIX system. No matter which way your system works, the printing process follows the same general pattern. First, you *format* the data to be printed, so that it is meaningful visually and so that the printer will understand how to print it. The formatted version of the file, referred to as the *print job,* is sent to the printer, where it becomes a *print request,* with its own ID number.

*D*ifferent Ways to Print with UNIX

Different kinds of printing will require slightly different ways of formatting and sending data. Before you start to print, then, identify which type of printing is in effect on your system. Depending on how your system has been set up, you may do local printing, spooled printing, or direct printing.

Local Printing

If you have a printer connected directly to your terminal, you can do *local printing.* Your UNIX system, if it is configured for local printing, will look more or less like the system in Figure 6.1.

This setup can be very inconvenient on a system that has only one printer. Often, everyone on the system wants to print things, and

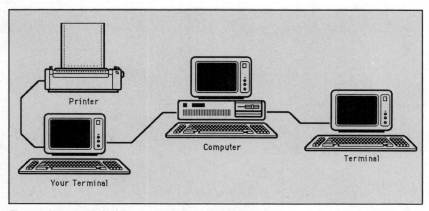

Figure 6.1: *A UNIX system set up for local printing*

sometimes they all seem to want to print things at once. On the other hand, local printing works fairly well if there are several printers, each of which is connected to a user's terminal. If your system does have local printers, learn the special print command devised for them; you might want to write the command down or put it in your hints file so you don't forget it. Use the command each time you want to print, and wait until your print job is finished before trying to work at your terminal again.

Spooled Printing

Spooled printing allows all users to send print requests to the computer from their terminals, and nobody has to stop working as printing proceeds. In this setup, the computer takes care of all the print jobs for you. It uses a program called a *spooler,* which comes from *s*imultaneous *p*eripheral *o*perations *on-l*ine. It refers to a way of sharing hardware devices. As far as printing is concerned, a spooler is simply a utility that puts different print jobs in a waiting line and "spools" them one by one to the printer.

The waiting line is called a *queue,* and your job is added to the queue as soon as you send it. The computer holds it in its memory with other print jobs, then sends it when the preceding jobs are done. You don't have to worry about when they are done. And you don't have to wait while your job is in the queue, or while it prints: you can go right on working. The spooled printing setup looks like Figure 6.2. The spooler itself is not an object you can see, but it is shown as an abstract object inside the computer.

This setup is great if your system's computer has the power and the memory to handle several print jobs and all of the users' other work at the same time. If people do lots of printing on your spooled system, you should also have a fast, reliable printer such as a laser printer.

Direct Printing

Direct printing is not recommended for most UNIX systems. Its setup is similar to the spooled one: the printer is connected to the computer, but instead of being queued, your print requests bypass the spooler and go directly to the printer. This setup looks like Figure 6.3.

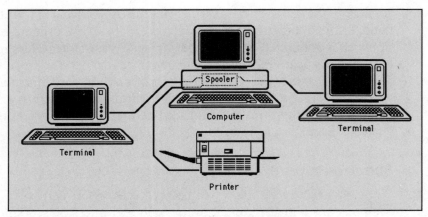

Figure 6.2: A UNIX system set up for spooled printing

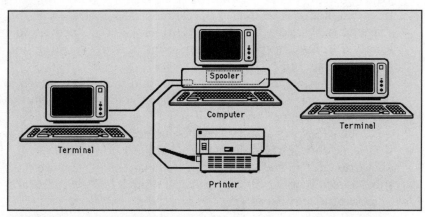

Figure 6.3: A UNIX system set up for direct printing (not recommended)

This type of printer setup is not recommended for multiuser systems because two print requests can be sent to the printer at the same time. If this happens, the printer attempts to print both files at once, and it either stops printing or prints out a jumbled mess.

If you are working on a small system, however, you can use direct printing as long as you make sure only one user sends a print request at a time. Direct printing often requires specialized commands. See your system administrator or ask an experienced user what the commands are for direct printing on your system.

The rest of this chapter deals with the recommended printing setup: spooled printing.

Preparing a File for Printing

Before you send a file to the printer, you format it. You can send an unformatted file, such as the calendar file you created with vi. It will print out, but it won't be pretty; if it's more than a page long, it will print right past the bottom of the first page and onto the top of the second one, with no top or bottom margins. You may wind up with lines cut in half at the end of the page. And there aren't any page numbers, so you can get the pages mixed up. If your printer uses fan-folded paper that feeds continuously out of a box, you can leave the printout all attached together, but this makes it hard to handle.

It's much nicer to have a neatly formatted printout, with a page number and a header at the top of each page, identifying the contents of the file that you have printed. The following procedure explains how to format a file in this way.

1. Move to the right directory.

If you want to print the calendar file you created by following the procedures earlier in this book, use the **cd** command to return to your home directory. Then enter **lf** to list the files in it, and make sure your calendar file is still there.

2. View the file to make sure it is ready to print.

Use vi to read the file and correct any mistakes in it before you commit it to paper. For example, enter **vi calendar** and look at all the dates in the file. Remove any lines with dates that are already in the past, and add new lines for dates coming up in the future. Correct typographical errors, too.

If you want to add a bunch of lines to make sure your calendar file is more than a page long, you can use the **yy** and **p** commands to yank 10 or 15 lines of your file and put them down at the bottom of it; use the **p** command more than once if you need to in order to wind up with at least 60 lines in the file. I just yanked a bunch of reminder lines of my sample calendar file and put them on again at the end. If you need to refresh your memory about editing with vi, see Chapter 2, "Writing and Editing Text with vi."

When you are completely satisfied with the contents of your file, save it and quit vi with the **ZZ** command.

3. Format the file.

The **pr** command lets you *pr*epare a file so it will print out properly. It does *not* send the file to the printer, as you might expect from the two letters, pr.

If you enter

pr calendar | more

the file appears on the screen, formatted into numbered pages, with a nice header that tells the file name and the time it was formatted. You don't have to pipe the output through the **more** command, but if you don't, the formatted file scrolls by on the screen so fast you don't get a chance to admire it. The beginning of the first page of my formatted calendar file looks like this:

Jul 5 14:49 1991 calendar Page 1

4/10/91 Take out the garbage
4/14/91 Put water in car radiator
4/17/91 Take out the garbage
4/18/91 Pay Louise for piano lesson
4/19/91 Scottish dance class
4/24/91 Take out the garbage
5/1/91 Take out the garbage

Notice that the header gives the date and time the file was last modified, the name of the file, and then the page number. The contents of the file start a couple of lines after that, and continue for a few screens. If you use the spacebar to scroll through the file, you see that there is a break of a few spaces after about 58 lines. Then the header appears again, signalling the start of page 2. The rest of the contents of the file are printed on the second page. In my sample there are only a few lines left.

The following sections explain different ways to specialize your file's format.

Format a file's contents into two columns.   If you have a file with all short lines running down the left side of the display, you can save paper by printing the file in two-column format. My calendar file fits that description, so I'll use the **-2** option with **pr**. If I enter

pr -2 calendar | more

the result is something like Figure 6.4.

```
Jul  5  14:49  1991  calendar  Page  1



4/10/91 Take out the garbage        6/26/91 Take out the garbage
4/14/91 Put water in the car radi  6/26/91 Take out the garbage
5/17/91 Take out the garbage        6/26/91 Take out the garbage
4/18/91 Pay Louise for piano less  6/26/91 Take out the garbage
4/19/91 Scottish dance class        6/26/91 Take out the garbage
4/24/91 Take out the garbage        6/26/91 Take out the garbage
```

Figure 6.4: *Using* **pr** *to format a two-column printout*

The lines from the beginning of the file are still on the left side, but another column has appeared on the right side of the screen, with the yanked reminder lines that I added to build the file up to a page.

Notice that the page is divided evenly between the two columns, even though the left column needed more space. The two long lines in the left column have been cut short to fit in the column. If you want to force **pr** to make room for long lines in the left column, you can add the additional **s** option **(pr -2s)** with **calendar** to format the file, but this option makes for ragged columns, which are hard to read. It is better to edit long lines to shorten them in this case, or to print out the file in a standard one-column format.

Replace the file name in the header.   Use the **-h** *"header"* option to put a descriptive title in the header of your printout instead of the file's name. Since "calendar" doesn't describe the contents of my calendar file the way I'd like, I can replace it by formatting the file like this:

pr -2h "Daily Reminders" calendar | more

The header of the formatted file will now read

Jul 5 14:49 1991 Daily Reminders Page 1

If the title has more than one word, you must enclose it in quotes, so the **pr** command doesn't interpret the second word as a file name. I enclose the title in quotes no matter how short it is—that way I never forget.

Double-space a file. If the text of a file is hard to read because the lines are too close together, or if you want to write notes between each line on the hard copy, format the file with the **-d** option to double-space the printout. For instance, I can combine options as follows:

pr -2dh "Daily Reminders" calendar | more

The file will appear on the screen with the text in two aligned columns, double-spaced. The new title appears in the header; and since my file is now longer than a page again, the header appears on both pages.

Notice that the **-h** option is added to the command after both other options, so the title can be entered as the first argument to **h**. You enter the name of the file to be printed immediately after the header title, separated from it by a space. It does not matter what order the **2** and **d** options are entered in, but they both have to appear before the **h** option so that you can put the title and the file name in their proper places.

Printing a Formatted File

After you have formatted your file, it's a relatively simple matter to send the file to the printer, as long as your system is using the standard spooler utility, **lp**. Check with your system administrator or an experienced user. Your system may use the lpr spooler; in that case, just substitute the **lpr** command for the **lp** command wherever it appears in this chapter.

If you find that some other customized print commands are used to print vi files on your system, use these commands instead of the **lp** command. If you produce files with applications that require special printing commands, such as the **l** command in the mail program, use the commands required by those applications (see "Printing from Applications" later in this chapter). The procedure below applies only to printing standard vi text files, formatted only with the **pr** command, and sent to the printer by an **lp** spooler or a similar spooler.

1. Print out a formatted copy of a file.

In the same way you pipe output of the **pr** command to your screen through the **more** command, you can pipe your file to **lp**. Replace **more** with **lp** and the formatted file will go to the printer. For example, if I want to print my calendar file, formatted as described in the last section, I can enter

pr -2dh "Daily Reminders" calendar | lp

When you press the Return key, there is a pause, usually a very brief one, and then a request ID message appears. It looks something like this:

request id is lab-8033 (standard input)

This is just the identification number of your print request, and the short name of the printer ("lab" in the example) that is printing it. Your system prompt reappears, indicating that the spooler is taking care of the printing process, so you can go back to work. If your file was a short one—less than ten pages—and there aren't lots of other users sending long files to the printer, you should be able to go pick up the printed copy of your file in a few minutes. If you haven't found out where the printer is yet, ask the system administrator or an experienced user. Mention the printer name or abbreviation that appeared in the request ID message.

If your file is a long one and you want to find out how the printer is doing, or if you want to cancel printing, you'll need to know the request ID number of your print job. Write the number down on a scrap of paper or memorize it.

Print two copies of a file.   If you want to print out two copies of your prepared file, you can add the option to the end of the whole command, so it becomes:

pr -2dh "Daily Reminders" calendar | lp -n2

This command will print out two copies of each page of the file. Although this is a simple way to make two copies of a short file, don't use it to make a copy of a long file, or to make numerous copies of a file. A printer is no substitute for a copying machine, and it is considered the height of bad manners on most UNIX systems to tie up a printer by making copies unnecessarily.

Specify a printer other than the default one.   If you have more than one printer on your UNIX system, your print jobs will automatically go to the default printer set up by your system administrator. If this printer is far away from your desk, or if lots of people are always printing out long jobs on it, you can direct your print job to another printer with the **-d** *printername* option with the **lp** command. The **d** stands for *d*estination. For example, if I want to send my sample print job to a printer called "doc" that is in my documentation department, I can enter the command:

pr -2dh "Daily Reminders" calendar | lp -ddoc

My print job will be printed by the nearby documentation department printer rather than the default printer (lab). I won't have to run all the way over to the lab printer and hang around waiting for all those long engineering department print jobs.

Ask to be notified when your print job finishes.   If you send a long job to the printer and want to know when it is done, you can add the **-m** option to the **lp** command:

pr -2db "Daily Reminders" calendar | lp -mddoc

and the spooler will mail you a note when printing is finished. Just check your mail for a message from a user called "lp." The contents of the message will look something like this:

Message 1:
From lp Fri Jul 5 15:26:54 1991

To: tomc
Date: Fri Jul 5 15:26:58 1991

printer request lab-8033 has been printed on printer doc

If you don't want to wait for a mail message, use the **-w** option with the **lp** command instead of **-m**. It writes the message directly to your terminal screen the instant the print job is finished. (This only works if you or your system administrator has set up your system so you can receive write messages from other users: see Chapter 10 for more information.)

2. Check the status of your print job.

If you haven't used the **-m** or **-w** options with **lp** as described above, or if you've been waiting an unusually long time to receive word that your file is finished, you can use the **lpstat** command to find out the status of your print request. If you have sent only one print request, just enter **lpstat** at the system prompt, without any arguments. If your job is being printed, you will see a message like this:

lab-8034 tomc 2300 Jul 5 15:00 on lab

Beginning at the left, this message tells the request ID number of your job, your login name, the number of characters to be printed, the date and time the print request was made, and where the print job is. If you don't see any message after giving the **lpstat** command, it means your print job is done already.

If you get a message indicating that your job is waiting in the queue, you can enter **lpstat -o** to get a listing of the queue. It will look something like this:

lab-8032 naomic 95936 Jul 5 14:57 on lab
lab-8033 davex   1842   Jul 5 14:59
lab-8034 tomc   2300   Jul 5 15:00

In this sample, I can see that Naomi has a pretty big print request going through (95936 characters), but when the printer gets done with it, Dave's little job (1842 characters) will only take a moment to print out. Then mine will get printed. Unless one of these files has some intricate graphics in it, my file will probably get printed out in less than five minutes.

3. Stop a print job.

If you need to stop printing for some reason, use **cancel** at the system prompt. If you have sent more than one job to the printer, enter the request ID number as an argument. For example, if I had sent two different jobs to print, and then wanted to cancel just the calendar printing job, I could enter

cancel lab-8033

The printer would stop printing the calendar, but would print any other ones I had sent.

4. Collect the printout of your file at the printer.

This seems obvious, but first you have to know where the printer is, and then you have to pick up your printout before you forget that it's waiting for you at the printer. If you work on a large system with numerous printers, find out from your system administrator or an experienced user which printer is the default one for you. Pick up all printouts soon after they are completed. This prevents jobs from piling up around the printer, and it decreases the chances that your job will get lost in the shuffle.

Printing from Applications

If you work with a special word processing, spreadsheet, or database application, you have to follow the specific printing procedure the application requires. Although every application has different commands for printing, in general, there are three steps you need to take before you can get a hard copy of the application's output.

1. Format the data or text.

This can mean anything from paginating text to making three-dimensional pie graphs out of spreadsheet data. Read the application's documentation and get help from an experienced user if you don't understand the formatting tools of the application. Some applications, such as e-mail, do the formatting automatically.

2. Preview the formatted output.

Most applications provide a way to see what you have formatted. There may be a "Preview" command, or a "View" option. Use the command or option; you can save a lot of paper and time spent running back and forth to the printer. If there are mistakes or elements of the formatted data or text that you think you could improve, redo the formatting and preview the output a second time before printing.

3. Give the appropriate print command.

In most applications, the print command is obvious; if it is not a choice in a prominently displayed menu on the screen, it is usually a simple command. In the e-mail program, the **l** *messagenumber* command does the trick. In many applications, the word **print** is all it takes. Some print commands, however, are not so obvious. You may have to ask your system administrator or a user who has had experience with the application about these.

When you complete your print command, you see the request ID number on your screen in most applications. This message tells you that your job is on its way to the printer.

Troubleshooting

I don't get a request ID message when I use the lp command.

You probably are not connected to the lp spooler, or the spooler is temporarily out of order, or your system doesn't have a default printer. See your system administrator.

I get a request ID message, but nothing is coming out of the printer.

Either something is wrong with the printer, or someone has sent a job to the printer that the printer can't print out.

Check the simplest thing first. See if there is paper in the printer's paper tray, or feeding into the printer from the paper box if you have fan-folded paper. Learn how to replenish the paper supply on your printer. There are so many different types of printers and paper trays I can't tell you how yours works, but I can describe the procedure in general.

If you have an empty paper tray, remove it, take off the lid if there is one, put in a stack of paper that fills the tray to the full mark, then replace the lid, replace the tray, and check the little lights on the side of the printer to make sure it is working again.

If you have run out of fan-folded paper, turn the printer off, open a new box of paper, pull the end of the paper out carefully, and feed it into the back of the printer. Turn the roller and, if necessary, adjust the positions of the paper-feeding wheels so the paper feeds smoothly into the printer with the page-break perforations lined up horizontally. Align a page-break with the marks on the printer for the beginning of a page, and turn the printer on again.

If your printer is not out of paper, check the little lights on the side to make sure it is on and working properly. If it isn't on, turn it on. If a light indicates that it is not working, contact your system administrator. If there is a light that blinks when the printer is working on a job, and that light just keeps blinking even though nothing is getting printed, then somebody has sent a "problem" job that is holding up the printer. Use the **lpstat -o** command to find out what is being printed, and if it doesn't come out soon, ask the sender of that print job to cancel it.

If there are no jobs being printed, the spooler may be temporarily out of order. Ask your system administrator to restart the spooler.

Only part of my print job came out, then the printer stopped.

Either the paper jammed in the printer, or you have something in your file that the printer can't print. Check the printer, then ask an experienced user or the system administrator for help in fixing the jam if that is the problem. If you are sure the paper is feeding properly, and the printer is still getting stuck on something in your file, cancel your print request, then edit the file to make sure it doesn't have some odd unprintable character in the text. You will have to check with other users to learn what characters might jam the printer, but things like control characters are often the culprits.

Command Summary

COMMAND	DESCRIPTION
cancel	Stops current print job.
lp *filename*	Prints named file. May be used without arguments if output from pr command is piped to lp command.
lp -n2 *filename*	Prints two copies of named file.
lp -d *printername* *filename*	Prints named file on named printer if more than one printer is on the system.
lp -m *filename*	Prints named file; notifies creator when finished.
lpstat	Reports status of current print job.
pr -2 *filename*	Prepares named file in 2-column format.
pr -d *filename*	Prepares named file with double-spacing.
pr -h *"header"*	Prepares named file with new name in header.

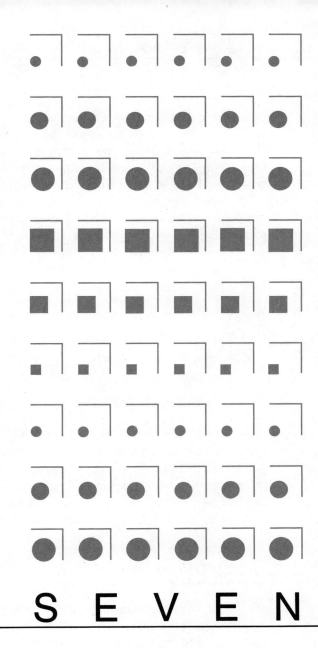

S E V E N

**Using Menus
and Windows:
Office Portfolio**

This chapter introduces a convenient way for you to interact with your UNIX system: a *menu* and *window* interface called Office Portfolio, which allows you to choose options from a menu, rather than having to write them from memory at the system prompt. The work you do and the information you see appears in windows, which keep things organized visually. In Office Portfolio, the windows appear on a *desktop*—a basic screen—with menus at the top of the screen.

First, you'll learn how to start Office Portfolio, if your system doesn't automatically start it for you. Then you'll see how to use the Desktop to:

- Use utilities
- Start applications
- Send electronic mail
- Use your daily events calendar
- Exit Office Portfolio

For more information on these subjects, see the Office Portfolio Quick Access Guide and other Office Portfolio documentation. If you have a different menu and window interface, you can still use the information in this chapter to learn the basic principles of using menus and windows, and then refer to the specific documentation for your interface to learn the details.

Starting Office Portfolio

Your UNIX system may be set up so that the Office Portfolio desktop appears automatically when you log in. If so, go on to the next section to learn about the Desktop.

If you see the system prompt when you finish logging in, start Office Portfolio by typing **op** and pressing Return. When you press the Return key, copyright information for Multiview (a windowing program) and Office Portfolio are displayed on the screen, and then the Office Portfolio desktop appears, as shown in Figure 7.1. Some of the details on your Desktop may be different, but the general layout should be similar.

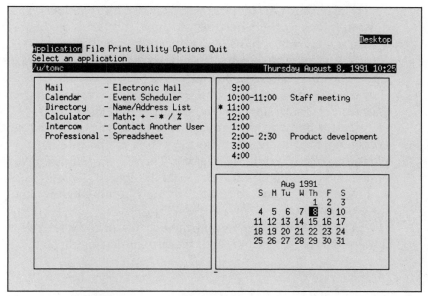

Figure 7.1: *The Office Portfolio Desktop*

About the Desktop

At the top of the Desktop is the menu: a row of options arranged across the top of your screen. The first option, **Application**, should be highlighted.

Under the menu line is a description line, telling you that if you choose the **Application** option, you will be able to select an application.

In the upper-right corner of the screen there is a context indicator that tells you where you are or what you are doing. You are looking at the Desktop, so it says Desktop.

Below the menu and description lines there is a bar that runs across the screen in reverse video. If you have a light-colored screen, the bar is dark; if you have a dark screen, the bar is light. This bar divides the menu from the windows below. The absolute path from the root directory to your working directory appears at the left end of the divider bar. In Figure 7.1, the path to my home directory, /u/tomc, is shown. The current date and time are displayed at the right end of the bar.

The bottom part of the screen is divided into windows. Your windows may look a little different from mine; it depends on the way your system administrator has set up Office Portfolio for you.

The window on the left side of the screen contains a list of the applications you can use. Your list may be longer or shorter than the one shown, but you will probably have the Directory application, Mail, the Calendar, and other applications, such as Professional.

The window in the top-right corner of the screen is the daily events window; it shows a short synopsis of the meetings or other plans on your schedule for the day. There is an asterisk next to the hour that is coming up; for example, in Figure 7.1 the time is 10:25 and the asterisk is next to 11:00. The view in this window changes as the day goes on.

The window in the bottom-right corner of the screen shows the days of the current month, with the current day highlighted.

Using Menus, and Windows

This section gives a brief tour of the Desktop and what you can do with it. The procedures will introduce you to each of the different elements of Office Portfolio, and tell you how to get in and out of them.

If there are shortcuts, they are described at the end of the steps that they apply to.

1. Move the highlight to different options.

To see what the different options in a menu do, use the arrow keys to move the highlight. The description line changes each time you move to a new option. If you press → a few times to move the highlight to the last option on the right (**Quit**), and then press → again, the highlight skips back to the first option, **Application**.

When you select an option, the screen changes. Usually, new choices are offered to you. Some options present a point-and-pick list of items to choose. Some options show you another menu. Some options open a form with fields that you can fill in with values. Let's select an option, to practice working with different choosing devices.

2. *Select the* Utility *option.*

You can select a menu option by moving the highlight to it, then pressing the Return key. This is the best approach if you are still learning what the different options in the menu do.

For example, if you highlight the **Utility** option and press the Return key, a point-and-pick list of utilities is displayed, with the highlight on the first one. Your list of utilities might be different than mine, but it probably contains some of the ones shown in Figure 7.2.

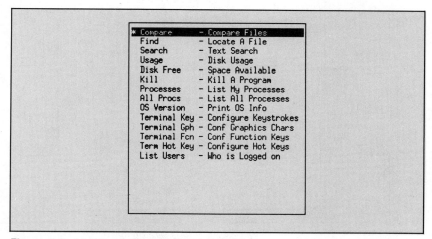

Figure 7.2: *A Utility option point-and-pick list*

If you know what an option in a menu does, you can enter the first letter of the option to select it. The option takes effect immediately; you don't have to move the highlight and press the Return key. For instance, from the first menu on the Desktop, enter **u**. The Utility point-and-pick list will be displayed immediately.

3. *Select an item from a point-and-pick list.*

In the Utility point-and-pick list, you can move the highlight with ↓ and ↑ until it is on a utility you want to use. For example, if you have the **List Users** option in your list and you want to see who is on the system, move the highlight down to **List Users** and press Return.

If you know the item you want in a point-and-pick list and are sure you want to select it, you can enter the first letter of the item. It will be selected immediately. For instance, to select the **List Users** option, enter l (an "el") without moving the highlight. The List Users window shown in Figure 7.3 appears. You may recognize the list; it's the same one you'd get if you used the **who** command at the system prompt.

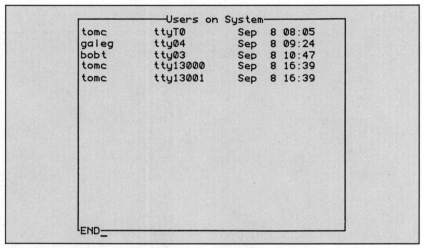

```
                  ─Users on System─
  tomc        ttyT0        Sep  8 08:05
  galeg       tty04        Sep  8 09:24
  bobt        tty03        Sep  8 10:47
  tomc        tty13000     Sep  8 16:39
  tomc        tty13001     Sep  8 16:39




  └END─
```

Figure 7.3: *Window displayed by the List Users utility*

There are a couple of hitches to using the first-letter shortcut in point-and-pick lists. If more than one item begins with the same letter, the highlight moves to the first. You must enter the same key again to move the highlight to the other items that begin with the same letter, then press the Return key when the item you want is highlighted. Also, the first-letter trick doesn't work in point-and-pick lists of files and directories.

4. Close the window with Return or Escape.

If the window brought up by the **List Users** command has an **END** sign at the bottom, you can press the Return key to close the window and return to the Portfolio desktop. If the list of users is long, you can use ↓ and ↑ to scroll through it, or press the Escape key to close the window. The Utility list appears.

5. Close a point-and-pick list without selecting an item.

If you open a point-and-pick list and then decide you don't want to select any of the items in it, press the Escape key to return to the menu where you were before opening the list. Now that you're back in the Utility list, for example, press the Escape key. The Utility point-and-pick list closes and returns you to the Office Portfolio Desktop.

6. Select Options from the Desktop menu, then select Reminders from the Options menu.

Either move the highlight to **Options** and press the Return key, or enter **o** to select it. A new menu appears at the top of the screen, as shown in Figure 7.4.

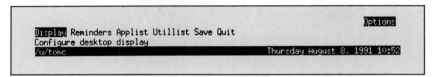

Figure 7.4: *The Options menu*

Select **Reminders**, either by moving the highlight to Reminders and pressing Return, or by entering **r**. The Configure Reminders form opens in the middle of the screen, with yes or no fields for appointment and mail reminders, and a field for specifying how many minutes of warning you want before an appointment.

If you know the options you are going to select in two successive menus, you can enter the first letters of both options at once. For example, if you are looking at the Desktop menu, and want to select **Options** and then **Reminders**, you can enter **or** to go directly to the Configure Reminders form.

7. Make choices in a form.

The default or formerly selected options and the fields in any form are enclosed in brackets. The first option or field is highlighted when the form appears. Use the arrow keys, or the spacebar and Backspace key to move the highlight between two options. Press the Return key to make a choice and move on to the next one. If there are numbers in a field and you want to change them, enter new ones and then press the Return key. Use the ↑ to back up to a previous field if you change your mind.

For example, in the Configure Reminders form shown in Figure 7.5, you can choose not to receive reminders of appointments by moving the highlight to the **no** option with → and then pressing the Return key. If you do this, the highlight skips the field for specifying how many minutes of warning you want, and goes directly down to the new mail line. If you choose to continue receiving appointment reminders, you can enter numbers to replace the **30** shown as the default, and press the Return key to move to the new mail reminder options.

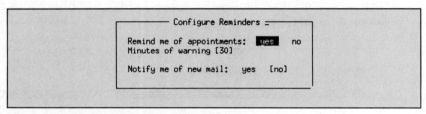

Figure 7.5: *The Configure Reminders form*

You can choose to be notified of new mail by selecting **yes** instead of the default **no** option in the last line of the form. If you want to keep the default setting, so you don't get interrupted in your work every time a new mail message arrives at your system mailbox, just press the Return key when the highlight is on **no**.

8. Close a form.

There are two ways to close a form and accept the values you have changed in it. If you work your way down to the bottom of the form, use the Return key. If you only want to change some of the values and options in the upper part of a form, use **Ctrl-X** (while holding the Control key down, press **x**).

For instance, when you press the Return key to make the last choice in the Configure Reminders form, the form closes and you return to the Options menu. If you want to change only the appointment warning time, enter **Ctrl-X** after doing so and the form closes. The changes you have made take effect for your current session of Office Portfolio, and you return to the Options menu. This method of closing a form is very useful on longer forms.

If you make some changes in a form and then decide you want to go back to the defaults, or if you open a form and decide you don't want to change anything, just press the Escape key to close the form and return to the menu you were in before you opened it.

For example, if you use the Escape key to abandon your changes in the Configure Reminders form after changing the appointment reminder field to **no,** the form closes and you return to the Options menu. You will get appointment reminders, as before.

9. Save changes for future sessions.

If you make changes in the Configure Reminders form and want to keep them in effect for future Office Portfolio sessions, save them when you close the window. At the Options menu, select **Save**. You are returned to the Desktop. If you quit the Desktop, then return to it again, your changes will still be in effect.

If you want the changes you made to stay in effect for the current Office Portfolio session only, select **Quit** in the Options menu, and you will return to the Desktop.

If there is no **Quit** option in a menu, you can use the Escape key to move to the next menu up. In fact, if you are ever stuck in a window, form, list, or menu where you don't want to be, try the Escape key. It often returns you to your previous situation.

Starting an Application in Office Portfolio

Use the following procedure to start up any application that is listed in the Applications window. If an application you need does not appear in the window, see your system administrator and ask if you can add the application to your list.

1. Select Application from the Desktop menu.

Move the highlight to **Application** and press Return, or enter **a** to select it. The whole Applications window becomes a point-and-pick list, with the first application highlighted, as shown in Figure 7.6.

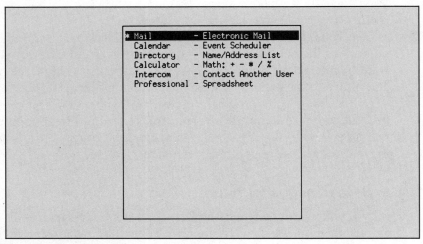

Figure 7.6: *An application list*

2. Select an application.

You can use ↓ to move the highlight down through the list to the application you want. You can also enter the first letter of the application, and it will start. In the sample application list shown in Figure 7.6, if you wanted to start the Calculator application, you would have to press **c** twice to bypass the Calendar and highlight the Calculator. Then you would have to press Return to select it.

After you select the application, a window opens, covering the desktop entirely.

3. Exit from an application.

Each application has a different procedure or command for exiting. See the application's documentation for further information. When you exit successfully, the Office Portfolio Desktop appears.

For example, if you are using Professional, you select the **Quit** option in the main menu, then save and name the current worksheet file if necessary. When you finish doing these things, the Professional window closes, and the Office Portfolio Desktop appears.

Using Office Portfolio Mail

You can create and read e-mail messages in Office Portfolio, just as you can from the system prompt. The only difference is that you carry out the various mail functions using menus and windows. The messages you send can be read by users who invoke mail from the system prompt, and you can read letters they create from the system prompt.

Use the following procedure to start the Mail program if you are looking at the Office Portfolio desktop.

1. Start Mail from the Desktop.

Either move the highlight to the **Application** option and press the Return key, or enter **a** to select it. The Applications point-and-pick list becomes active, with the first application highlighted. On our system, Mail is the first application, so the list comes up with it highlighted. This may not be the case on your system.

Use the ↓ key to move the highlight down to **Mail** and press Return, or enter **m** to select it directly. The opening screen of the Mail program appears, as shown in Figure 7.7.

The message list shows the number of each message you have received, who it came from, when it was sent, how many lines of text it contains, and what the subject is.

The options in the mail menu let you read your mail, create new mail messages, and save, delete, undelete, or print messages you have received. You can also set options that control how mail behaves, and quit the mail program.

2. Select Read from the Mail menu.

Enter **r** to select **Read**. The first message in the list becomes highlighted, the Mail menu disappears, and a prompt appears in the description line asking you to enter a message number.

3. Select a message to read.

Move the highlight to the message you want to read and press the Return key, or enter the number of the message and press the Return key. The Read menu appears, and the first screenful of the message you chose. For example, if I chose message number 6 from the list in Figure 7.7, the header and the first part of the message would appear under the Read menu as shown in Figure 7.8.

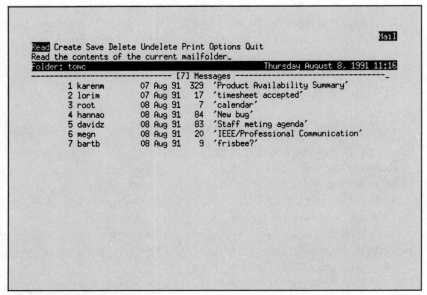

Figure 7.7: *The opening Mail screen*

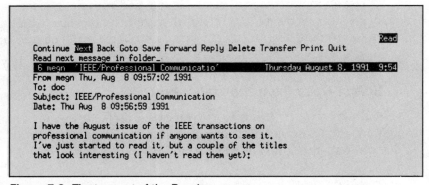

Figure 7.8: *The top part of the Read screen*

The header of the message, which appears just under the reverse video divider bar, tells who the message is from, when it was sent, to whom it was addressed, what the subject is, and when you received it.

If the message you selected in the message list is longer than one screenful, press the Return key to select **Continue** from the Read menu and read the rest of the message.

When you finish reading a message, the highlight moves automatically to the **Next** option. Just press the Return key again to read the next message.

If you want to see a previous message, use the **Back** option. If you want to skip some messages and read one that is further down the list, use the **Goto** option. When you select **Goto**, the message list appears and you can move the highlight to a message or enter its number, then press the Return key to select it. In later versions of Mail, a menu appears, with options for a new message, a message with the same subject, or any other message.

4. Dispose of your messages.

If you want to save a mail message, select the **Save** option and fill in the fields in the form that opens, specifying the file or Mail-Folder where you want to save the message, and whether you want to save the header as well as the text. Press **F3** (Function key 3) to see a list of available files or Mail-folders. Mail-folders are files that contain several mail messages. For more information on creating and using them, see the Office Portfolio documentation.

If you want to delete a message after reading it, select the **Delete** option. You can undelete the message at any time before quitting mail.

If you want to print a message, select the **Print** option. If you want to use a different printer than the default one, use the **Select** option in the Print menu. Then use the **Go** option to print the message.

You can carry out some of these functions from the Mail menu as well as from the Read menu. If you read all your messages first, then return to the message list in the opening Mail screen, just use the **Save, Delete**, and **Print** options in the Mail menu. The only risk in doing this is that you might forget that a message is important and delete it by mistake. If you tend to forget which messages need to be saved and which can be deleted, do your saving and deleting immediately after reading each message while you are still in the Read menu.

5. Forward a message to another user.

If you want to send a message you've received on to someone else, select the **Forward** option in the Read menu. A form appears, with fields for who you want to forward the message to, and who you want to send carbon copies to. There is also an option to edit the message before forwarding it. (See the following section for information on editing messages.)

6. Create a mail message.

From the Mail menu, move the highlight to the **Create** option and press Return, or enter **c** to select it. The Editing Header form appears, with the cursor in the Subject field, as shown in Figure 7.9.

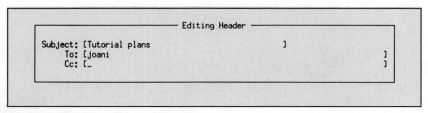

```
                          ─── Editing Header ───
    Subject: [Tutorial plans                           ]
         To: [joani                                              ]
         Cc: [_                                                  ]
```

Figure 7.9: The Editing Header form

Enter a meaningful, short subject in the **Subject** field; if it is longer than 27 characters, it might appear in a cut-off form in the message lists of users who are running the Mail program from the system prompt. Then press the Return key to move to the **To** field.

In the **To** field, enter the login names of the user or users you want to send the mail to. If you can't remember a user's login name, press **F3** for a list of users on your system. Press the Return key to move to the **Cc** field.

Enter the login names of the users you want to send "carbon copies" of the message to in the **Cc** field. When you press the Return key, the form closes and the cursor appears in a blank screen, ready for you to write the text of your message. A note in the description line tells you that you are editing text, and that you can bring up menus by pressing the Escape key.

Type in the text of your message, remembering to press the Return key to end each line about two-thirds of the way across the screen.

To edit mistakes or make additions to the text, use the text editing keystrokes for Office Portfolio. The Backspace and arrow keys work the same as in vi, and some cursor movement keys such as **Ctrl-J, Ctrl-K, Ctrl-L,** and **Ctrl-H** are familiar relatives of vi keystrokes. For a complete list of the text editing commands for Mail, see the Command Summary at the end of this chapter.

7. Send the message.

Press the Escape key to see the Create menu when you finish writing your message. Then just press the Return key to select the **Deliver** option; it is already highlighted when the menu appears, as shown in Figure 7.10.

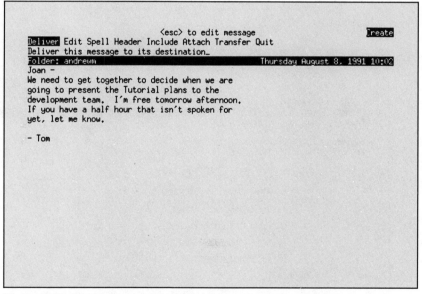

Figure 7.10: The Deliver option on the Create menu

Note that you can also use the Include option in this menu to include messages or files in the mail message you are creating. You can use the Header option to specify things like blind carbon copies and return receipt.

If you decide not to send the message, select the **Quit** option. A short form lets you either hold the message for future delivery or delete it.

If you decide at the last moment before delivering the message that you need to edit it, just press the Escape key; the cursor appears where you left it in the message text. You can use the **Edit** option for the same purpose, but it will invoke a different editor than the Office Portfolio one you have been using.

8. Reply to a mail message.

From the Read menu, move the highlight to the **Reply** option and press the Return key, or enter **r** to select it. A form appears, like the one shown in Figure 7.11, with fields that let you specify who will get your reply, and whether the original message will be included and indented in your reply.

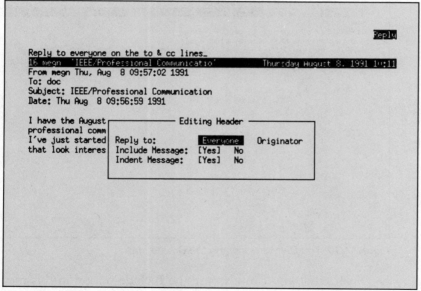

Figure 7.11: The Editing Header form for replying to a message

Choose **Everyone** if you want to send your reply to all of the users who received the message and carbon copies of it. Choose the **Originator** option if you want to reply to the sender only.

Choose to include the message if you want to comment on specific things in it, and you want to make sure people remember what you're commenting on. Choose to indent the message if you want to set it apart from your reply. Don't indent the message if it is wide enough to fill the screen: the indented version will probably have lines that overflow, which makes it hard to read.

Close the form by pressing the Return key after you make your last choice in it. If you don't want to change any of the default settings, enter **Ctrl-X** to close the form. The Mail program puts you in Edit mode, ready to create your reply. If you chose to include the original message, it appears on the screen.

You can enter your reply as described in step 6. If you include the original message in your reply, you can use **Ctrl-O** to intersperse your comments in the text of the original message. For a summary of the other editing commands you can use, see the Command Summary at the end of this chapter.

9. Send your completed reply.

When you finish entering the text of your reply, press the Escape key to bring up the Create menu. Then press Return to select the Deliver option, which is already highlighted.

10. Exit Mail.

To exit from the mail program, move the highlight to the **Quit** option in the Mail menu or enter **q**. The Office Portfolio Desktop reappears.

Using the Office Portfolio Calendar

The Calendar can help you keep track of daily events such as appointments, meetings, and deadlines. When you start Office Portfolio you see a short section of the calendar in the Daily Events window. This window is not to be confused with the Monthly Calendar window, which just shows the days of the month.

The following procedures describe how to start the Calendar program, how to view the calendar by day, week, or month, and how to add an event to your calendar, then edit or delete it.

1. Start Calendar.

From the Desktop, enter **ac** to select Application and then Calendar. The Calendar opening screen appears, with the day's events listed. A sample opening screen is shown in Figure 7.12.

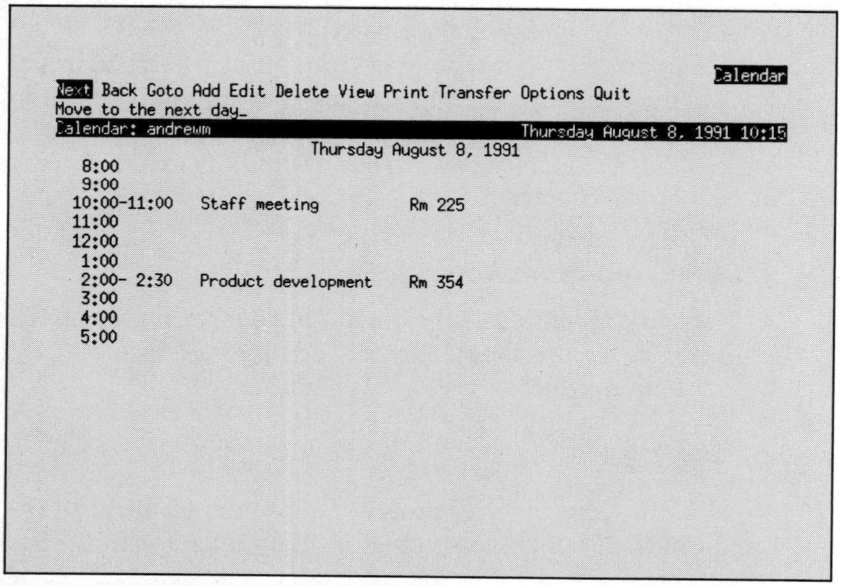

```
                                                              Calendar
 Next Back Goto Add Edit Delete View Print Transfer Options Quit
 Move to the next day_
 Calendar: andrewm                          Thursday August 8, 1991 10:15
                        Thursday August 8, 1991
     8:00
     9:00
    10:00-11:00    Staff meeting         Rm 225
    11:00
    12:00
     1:00
     2:00- 2:30   Product development    Rm 354
     3:00
     4:00
     5:00
```

Figure 7.12: The Calendar opening screen

Notice that the listing for each event shows the place where it takes place, as well as the time and the name of the event.

2. View previous and upcoming days.

If you want to see your schedule for tomorrow, move the highlight to the **Next** option and press the Return key, or enter **n**. If you want to see yesterday's events, select the **Back** option or enter **b**.

If you want to see the events for a day that is not within a few days of the present, move the highlight to the **Goto** option in the Calendar menu and press the Return key, or enter **g**. A three-month calendar appears at the bottom of the screen. You can use the arrow keys to move the highlight to any date shown. If you move to a date that is out of the visible range, the calendar scrolls to show the date you want.

You can also enter a date; it appears at the prompt above the divider bar. You can view daily events from 1900 to 2099. (If you find anything interesting going on in 1900, let me know!)

3. See weekly or monthly events calendars.

If you want to see a summary of your events for the current week, move the highlight to the **View** option in the Calendar menu and press the Return key, or enter **v**. Then press the Return key to select **Week** from the View calendar. To see a monthly summary of events, enter **m** to select **Month** from the View menu. You can scroll either calendar to see more events, using the arrow keys. Press the Escape key to close either the weekly or the monthly event calendar and return to the Calendar menu.

4. Add a calendar event.

From the Calendar menu, use the Next, Back, or Goto options to see the day on which you want to schedule an event. Then, from the Calendar menu again, select Add and Event by entering **ae**. The menu disappears, and the highlight appears in the **8:00** line of the day you selected.

Use the arrow keys to move the highlight to the line for the time of your event, then press the Return key. The Add form appears, with the cursor in the Duration field, as shown in Figure 7.13.

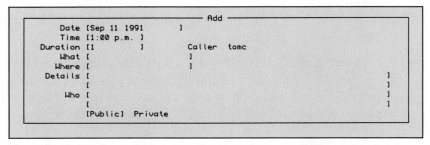

Figure 7.13: *The form you use to add an event to your daily events calendar*

The date and time of the event are already filled in, and the default duration of one hour is entered. Your name appears in the Caller field, because you are the one scheduling the event.

Enter a number of hours and minutes in the Duration field. Type a short description of the event in the **What** field, and press Return. If you don't have to add any details to the description, just press the Return key twice more to move to the **Who** field. If you are calling a meeting with other users and want to schedule the meeting for them as well as for yourself, enter their login names in the **Who** field, or choose them from the list you can see by pressing **F3**. If you are adding an event to your own calendar rather than calling a meeting with others, press the Return key twice to leave the **Who** field empty. If you don't want other users to know the nature of the event you are scheduling, choose the **Private** option at the bottom of the form. Otherwise, leave the **Public** option chosen. When you press the Return key after making this last choice, the Add form closes and the daily events calendar appears with the new events shown.

5. Change data for a scheduled event.

If you can see that there is an error in the way you scheduled the new event, or if there is a change in plans and you need to modify it, select the **Edit** option in the Calendar menu, by moving the highlight to **Edit** and pressing Return, or enter **e**. Then use the spacebar to move the highlight to the event you want to modify and press Return again. The Add form opens with the event's data shown in the fields. Use the Return key to accept data and move to the next field. Enter the correct data where needed, and either press the Return key until you move off the bottom of the form, or enter **Ctrl-X** to close the form and accept the data you entered.

6. Remove an event from your calendar.

If a meeting is cancelled or a deadline changed, remove the event by moving the highlight to the **Delete** option in the Calendar menu and pressing the Return key, or by entering **d**. Move the highlight to the event you want to delete if there are two or more events on the current day. Then press Return again. Another menu appears asking you to confirm the deletion. Move the highlight to the **Yes** option and press the Return key, or enter **y**. The daily events calendar reappears, without the event.

7. Exit Calendar.

To exit from the Calendar program, move the highlight to the **Quit** option in the Calendar menu and press the Return key, or enter **q**. Another menu appears; enter **y** to confirm that you want to leave the Calendar. The Office Portfolio desktop reappears.

Exiting Office Portfolio

To exit from the Desktop, move the highlight to the **Quit** option and press the Return key, or enter **q**. Another menu appears; enter **y** to confirm that you want to leave the Desktop. You can also exit more quickly by entering **qy**. Your system prompt appears.

Troubleshooting

The Control or arrow keys don't work as they should.

If you try to move the cursor with an arrow key and it doesn't work, try the keystroke command alternative given in the Command Summary. For instance, if the cursor doesn't move to the right when you press the → key, try **Ctrl-L**. If a Control keystroke doesn't work the way you expect it to, make sure you are in a mode that allows the Control keystroke.

If the simple solutions above don't fix your problem, see your system administrator. Your terminal may not be configured correctly, or your system may need a new capability file for your type of terminal. The terminal may not be able to deliver the keystroke function you want. Some terminals simply don't have all of the standard keystroke functions.

I can't move to a directory that is above the working one in the file system.

You cannot use the **cd** command to change to a directory above your working directory. In the Office Portfolio File window, you have to select the *../* directory at the beginning of the file listing in order to move to the next higher directory and list the files in it. To move to a directory that is far away in the hierarchy, you must select the *../* directory until you are at the root directory, then select directories in the root and lower directories to work your way down to the target directory. If you know the absolute path of a file you need, you can enter it and access the file directly.

Command Summary

COMMAND   DESCRIPTION

Cursor Movements:

Ctrl-B	Deletes characters to left (Backspace).
Ctrl-D	Moves you down one screenful.
Ctrl-E	Moves you to end of form.
Ctrl-H	Moves cursor left one character.
Ctrl-J	Moves cursor down one line.
Ctrl-K	Moves cursor up one line.
Ctrl-L	Moves cursor right one character.
Ctrl-N	Moves cursor to next word.
Ctrl-P	Moves cursor to previous word.
Ctrl-T	Moves cursor to top of screen or form.

Inserting and Deleting:

Ctrl-O	Opens a new line.
Ctrl-V	Puts you in and out of Overstrike mode.

COMMAND   DESCRIPTION

Inserting and Deleting:

Ctrl-W   Deletes a word.

Ctrl-Y   Deletes a line.

Delete   Deletes a character.

Other Functions:

Return   Selects option or accepts data in a field.

Space bar   Adds option to list of selections.

Ctrl-X   Executes form; close it and accept data.

Escape   Escape; exits a form without accepting new data.

F1   calls up Help.

F2   Exits form or application.

F3   Lists choices.

/   Puts you in menu mode.

!   Lets you enter system prompt commands.

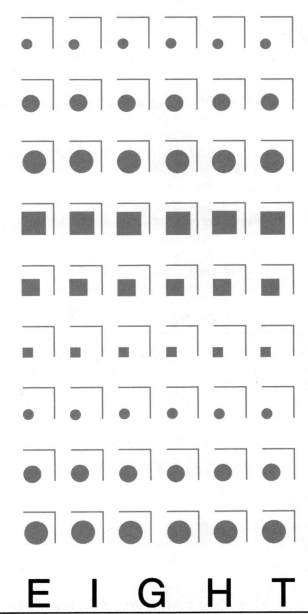

E I G H T

**Using
SCO UNIX
Applications**

In this chapter, you'll learn about the major applications packages available with SCO UNIX. Basic procedures are described for each application: how to start the application, enter data, print, save, and exit. If you make extensive use of an application program and need further information, you should consult the SCO UNIX documentation for that program.

If you are using a desktop menu program such as Office Portfolio, keep in mind that you will start each of the following applications from the Applications menu on that program's Desktop. Similarly, when you quit each of the following applications, you will be returned to the Desktop rather than to the system prompt.

Using Microsoft Word for UNIX

This section teaches you about word processing with Microsoft Word for UNIX. It describes what a word processor is and what you can do with it, and then briefly describes how to:

- Start Word

- Use the Word document screen and menu

- Get Help while using Word

- Create, save, and print text documents

- Exit Word

If you need more than basic information on any of these procedures, see the Microsoft Word for UNIX documentation.

Working with a Word Processor

A word processor is an application you can use to write, revise, and format text documents. You can create anything from short memos and reports to books, and you can put your text in any format from fine-print footnotes to oversize block-letter headings.

You have more power to edit and format text with a word processor than you have with a text editor like vi. To print a vi file in a special format, you have to use other applications, such as nroff or troff. A word processor can edit more than one line at a time, and usually provides ways to format words, lines, pages, or whole documents: magazine pages, book chapters, legal briefs, and outlines, to name a few. You can print your document with many different page styles and fonts, so that its appearance reflects its contents, and it appeals to your prospective audience.

You can also circulate word processed documents as software files. If you circulate a text file for review, you can use Word to track the reviewer's comments and mark your corrections of the text. You can also archive documents and backup copies of documents, so that all the users on your UNIX system can find them easily.

*S*tarting Word and Creating a New Document

Use the following procedure to begin writing a new text document with a name of your choice. You can use the same procedure to create a new document without a name, but you will have to name the document eventually, when you save it.

1. Start Word with the word filename command.

Just type **word**, a space, the name you want to give your document, and the Return key. It can be any name you want, with any combination of numbers and lower- and uppercase letters. The name cannot be more than ten characters long. For example, if I want to create a document named "prospects" I can type

word prospects

and then press Return.

If you make a mistake typing the command, you can use the backspace key to back up past the mistake and retype the command.

The copyright information for Word appears on the screen, and then a message appears:

File does not exist. Enter Y to create or Esc to cancel

Word is checking to make sure you want to create a new file with the name you entered.

2. Enter y to create the new file.

You can enter either an uppercase or lowercase **y** to confirm your choice of a filename. Word displays a document window, with the filename you entered in the lower-right corner and the cursor blinking in the upper-left corner. The window for my prospects file looks like Figure 8.1.

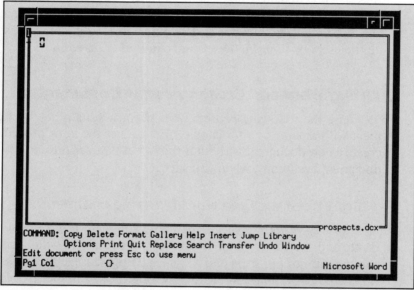

Figure 8.1: *The Word for UNIX document window*

Notice that Word adds the extension **.dcx** to the name of your file. This extension stands for *document* and it helps you to recognize a Word document file.

3. Begin typing to enter text.

You do not have to enter a command before you begin typing the text of your Word document. As you enter the text, the asterisk that marks the end of the file moves along with the cursor. You should not press Return at the end of each line of text; Word wraps the text to the next line for you. Only press Return at the end of paragraphs or other single elements of text. For more information on entering text, see the "Entering and Deleting Text" section later in this chapter.

4. Press the Escape key to access the command menu.

If you are entering text in Word and you want to use the commands in the menu at the bottom of the document window, press the Escape key. The first command, **Copy**, becomes highlighted.

To choose a different command, either use the arrow keys or the Tab key to move the highlight to the command you want, then press the Return key. When a command is highlighted, you can read a description of it on the message line that appears below the commands.

If you know what a command does, you do not have to highlight it to use it. You can enter the first letter of the command, and it will be executed immediately: you don't even have to press Return. As in Office Portfolio, you can also enter a series of first-letter commands, once you know your way around the command menus.

Starting Word and Loading an Existing Document

If you have a Word document file in your working directory, you can open it and begin editing it or adding new text to it. The file will have the .dcx extension if it was created with Word. You can use either of the following ways to start Word from the system prompt.

1. Start Word and get into an existing Word document.

From the system prompt, enter **word** *filename*, just as you would to start a new file. But instead of making up a new name, enter the name of the Word file you want to start. You do not have to enter the .dcx extension. For example, if I want to start word and get into my prospects.dcx file, I can enter

word prospects

and press the Return key.

The Word document window opens, with the name of the document in the lower-right corner, and the cursor under the first character of the existing text.

2. Start Word and
get into the last document you worked on.

If you have recently quit working on a Word document and want to return to it, enter

word -l

command at the system prompt. The document window opens with the name of the last file you loaded in the lower-right corner. The cursor appears under the last character you added or modified.

Creating and Editing Documents from Inside Word

If you have already been using Word to create a document and you want to create or edit a different one, use the following procedure.

1. Choose the Transfer Load *command from the menu.*

Press the Escape key to move the highlight to the command menu at the bottom of the screen. Then enter **tl** to choose the Transfer command and then the Load command.

2. Enter the name
of a new file and save the current document.

If you want to create a new file, enter a new name of 10 characters or less at the file name prompt, then press Return.

If you want to load an existing file, enter its name at the file name prompt. If you don't remember the name, press **F1** to list the available files and directories. Highlight the file you want, or highlight the directory with the file you want, and press Return.

If you have made changes to the document currently in the document window, Word asks if you want to save them; enter **y** to do so. If you are creating a new document, Word will tell you that the new file does not exist; enter **y** to create it, and the document window for your new document opens. If you are opening an existing document, Word puts you directly into the file.

*E*ntering and Deleting Text

This section describes how to enter text, how to insert new text in a document, and how to delete text when you make mistakes.

1. Enter text by typing.

To enter text in Word, you just type it. There is no need to enter an insert mode, as in vi. After you use a Control character or a command from the command menu, Word returns you automatically to insert mode. Whenever you see the cursor blinking in the document window, you can begin typing; text appears at the cursor's location. When you come to the end of a line, the text automatically wraps to the next line. Don't press Return until you reach the end of a paragraph.

2. Erase mistakes by backspacing over them.

If you make a mistake in a word, all you have to do is backspace over the incorrect characters and type them correctly. For example, if I type the word **remarkabel**, I can press the Backspace key twice from the end of the word, and then enter **le** to correctly spell *remarkable*.

3. Turn overtyping on and off with **F5***.*

If you make a mistake in the middle of a long word or passage, you can move back to the beginning of the mistake with the arrow keys, then press **F5** to turn on overtyping. This allows you to type over text, replacing old letters with new ones. Type the correct letters, then press **F5** again to turn overtyping off. Use → to move the cursor past the text you have already typed. For example, if I type **remrakable** I can press ← to move the cursor from the end of the word back to the **r** that is misplaced. Then I can press **F5** and enter **ar** to correct the spelling. After pressing **F5** again, I can use → to move back to the end of the word again.

4. Use the Delete key to delete extra letters.

If you accidentally enter extra letters in the middle of a long word or passage, you can use the Delete (Del) key to remove the letters. For example, if I type **remaaarkable**, I can press ← to move the cursor back to the second **a** in the word. Then I can press the Delete Key twice to remove the two extra letters, and use → to move the cursor back to the end of the word again.

5. Press the Return key to start a new paragraph.

You do not have to press the Return key at the end of each line of text you enter. You should use the Return key only to separate paragraphs. This is called a *hard return,* as opposed to the *soft returns* Word inserts automatically when it breaks your paragraph into visual lines. Depending on the setting for first line indentation (set with **Format Paragraph**), the next character you type after a hard return may or may not be indented.

Moving the Cursor Around the Text

You can move the cursor around within a document by using the arrow keys, or by using special Control-character combinations. To move the cursor with a Control character, hold the Control key (Ctrl) down, then press and release the other key indicated. If two other keys are indicated, hold the first down while holding the Control key down, then press and release the second key.

For example, to move the cursor down one line, you can either press ↓ or hold the Control key down as you type the **j** key (**Ctrl-J**). To scroll up one windowful, hold the Control key down, then press and release the **u** key (**Ctrl-U**). To move to the beginning of the document, hold down the Control key, then hold down the **c** key, then press and release the **u** key (**Ctrl-C-U**). Although uppercase letters are conventionally used to denote control keystrokes such as Ctrl-J and Ctrl-C-U, do not enter uppercase letters. It is hard enough to hold down the Control key; you don't have to hold down the Shift key, too!

Table 8.1 lists some of the most commonly used cursor-movement keystrokes.

Selecting Text

Before you can use some Word commands, such as **Copy**, **Delete**, and **Format Character**, you have to select text for the command to act

Table 8.1: *Cursor Movement Keys in Word for UNIX*

KEYSTROKE	CURSOR MOVEMENT
↑ *or* Ctrl-K	Up; to line above
↓ *or* Ctrl-J	Down; to line below
← *or* Ctrl-G	Left; to previous character
→ *or* Ctrl-L	Right; to next character
Home *or* Ctrl-T	To first character in line
End *or* Ctrl-E	To last character in line, or end of line
PgUp *or* Ctrl-U	Up one window
PgDn *or* Ctrl-D	Down one window
Ctrl-PgUp *or* Ctrl-C-U	To beginning of document
Ctrl-PgDn *or* Ctrl-C-D	To end of document

upon. Selected text is highlighted on the screen. You can select any amount of text, from a single character to the whole document. The character at the cursor is selected by default. You can extend a selection by using the Shift key and the arrow keys together. To make a large extension of a selection, press **F6**, use the cursor-movement keystrokes, then press **F6** again. Table 8.2 lists some of the most commonly used selection keystrokes.

Getting Help While Using Word

If you have difficulty understanding the effect of a command or how to complete a procedure while using Word, you can always read Word's Help screen for information and brief instructions.

If you need help on a specific command or field, move the highlight to the command or field. Then, before doing anything else, enter **Alt-H** (hold down **Alt** and press **h**). If you do not have an Alt key on your keyboard, enter **Ctrl-A-H**. These same keystrokes will give you help on editing text if the cursor is anywhere in the document window.

Table 8.2: *Selecting Text in Word for UNIX*

KEYSTROKE	TEXT SELECTED
F7	Previous word
F8	Next word
Shift-F7 *or* Ctrl-Z-F7	Previous sentence
Shift-F8 *or* Ctrl-Z-F8	Next sentence
F9	Previous paragraph
F10	Next paragraph
Shift-F9 *or* Ctrl-Z-F9	Current line
Shift-F10 *or* Ctrl-Z-F10	Whole document
Shift-arrow keys *or* Ctrl-Z-arrow keys	Extended block of text (for smaller extensions)
F6 *and cursor movement key*	Extended block of text (for larger extensions)

After reading the Help screen, press **e** to exit the Help screen and return to your work.

If the cursor is in the document window and you need help on general topic, use the following procedure.

1. Choose Help *from the command menu.*

Press the Escape key to access the command menu, then press **h** to see the Help window. Read the three screens of information on Help, pressing **n** to see the next screen when you finish reading each screenful.

2. Use the Help index to choose topics.

Press **i** to see the Help index. An alphabetized list of topics will appear. Use the arrow keys to move the highlight to the topic you need help with, then press Return.

3. Read the Help screens on a topic.

If there is more than one screen, you can press **n** to see the next screen or **p** to see the previous screen.

4. Exit from Help or return to the Help index.

When you have read the information on a Help topic, press **e** to exit and return to your work with Word, or press **i** to go back to the Help index again. When you exit Help, the cursor returns to its previous position in your text.

Saving Your Document

As you create a new text document or modify an existing one, your work is held temporarily in the computer's memory. This work can be lost in the case of a power surge or hardware problem. To prevent this catastrophe, you should save the document to the hard disk often as you work, and also save before you quit Word. The following procedure describes how to save a document in the current directory.

1. Choose Transfer Save from the command menu.

If you are editing text, press the Escape key to access the menu commands, then press **ts** to save the document. If you have named the file, Word displays the name in a file name field. The full pathname is shown, with the name of the document at the end, including its .dcx extension. For example, my prospects document appears as /u/tomc/Words/prospects.dcx in the filename field. If you are content with the name of your document file, press Return. If you want to enter a new name for the file, do so, and then press Return. Your cursor will return to its previous position in the text.

2. Name the document if you have not done so.

If the file name field is blank, enter a name of ten characters or less and press the Return key. The document is saved as a file with the name you entered, either in the working directory, or in the directory specified by the **Transfer Options** command. Your cursor returns to its previous position in the text of the document.

3. Fill out the summary sheet if necessary.

If this is the first time you have saved a new document, you might see a Summary Information display with fields for the title, author, operator, and so on. Fill in these fields if you need them, entering text in each field, and then using the Tab or arrow keys to move to the next field. When you have filled all the fields, press the Return key.

If you don't want to fill any of the fields, just press the Return key before entering any text.

In either case, your cursor returns to its previous position in the text.

*P*rinting Word Documents

If a printer that is configured for Word has been installed on your UNIX system, you can print Word documents with it. The following procedure prints out the document you're working on, according to settings made with the **Print Options** command.

1. Save the current document before printing it.

Save your document, so that you have a backup copy if your print request fails and your data is lost.

2. Check the printer to make sure it is ready to print.

Make sure there is paper in the printer and that it is turned on. If you have fan-fold paper, make sure the top of the first page is lined up with the print head.

3. Choose **Print Printer** *from the command menu.*

If you are editing the document, press the Escape key and enter **pp** for **Print Printer**. Your request is added to the queue of jobs waiting to be printed, just like any other print job, and Word displays the request ID message.

4. Cancel a print request with **Print Queue Cancel.**

If you send a print job to a spooled printer and then decide that you do not want to print it out, enter **pqc** from the command menu to cancel your print job. The cursor returns to its previous position in your document.

*E*xiting Word

When you have finished your word processing work, use the following procedure to leave Word and return to the system prompt.

1. Choose Quit *from the command menu.*

Press the Escape key if you are editing a document, then enter **q** to quit Word. If you have not changed anything in the document since you last saved it, the Word document window closes and the system prompt appears.

If you have made changes to the document since saving it, Word displays a message asking if you want to save the changes.

2. Enter y *to save changes if you need to.*

Word saves your modifications to the current document before allowing you to quit. This way you cannot accidentally lose your work, even if you forget to save it. When you enter **y** and press the Return key, one of three things happens. If you have named the file, either the system prompt returns, or a summary sheet appears. If you have not named the document file, Word displays the file name prompt.

3. Name the file if you have not done so.

Enter a filename of 10 characters or less and press the Return key.

4. Fill in the summary sheet if necessary.

If you have never saved the document before, you might see a Summary Information display with fields for the title, author, operator, and so on. Fill in these fields if you need them, entering text in each field, and then using the Tab or arrow keys to move to the next field. When you have filled the fields, press the Return key.

If you don't want to fill any of the fields, just press the Return key before entering any text.

In either case, when you press the Return key, the Word document window closes and the system prompt appears.

Using SCO Professional

This section teaches you to use SCO UNIX's spreadsheet application, SCO Professional. First, it defines spreadsheets in general, and then talks about what you can do with Professional. Then you'll learn how to:

- Start Professional
- Use the Worksheet screen and menu
- Get Help while using Professional
- Create, save, and print worksheets and graphs
- Exit Professional

If you need more information on any of these procedures, see the SCO Professional documentation.

Working with a Spreadsheet

A *spreadsheet* stores and reports numerical information in a row-and-column format. A *worksheet* is the electronic form of a paper spreadsheet. You can use worksheets for a wide variety of business purposes, from simple cost reports to complex budgets, loan analyses, and tax statements. A great advantage of a computer worksheet over a paper spreadsheet is that you can make entries that change depending on other entries, so that when you update one entry, the others are also updated automatically. This feature gives you the ability to predict the possible results of different situations. You can set up a worksheet that shows projected profits based on production costs, for instance, and then create several "what-if" situations, changing the production costs to see instantly what the effects will be on profits. You can save or print each projection, and enter actual costs as time goes on to determine which projection was the most accurate. You can display the spreadsheet information in graph form for improved clarity, and print out the graphs for presentations.

SCO Professional can also be used as a database, where each row is set up as a record and each column is a field. You can then enter, sort, query, and analyze the data in various ways.

Starting Professional and Creating a New Worksheet

Use the following procedure to display a blank worksheet screen, so you can begin to build a new worksheet.

1. Start Professional and display the worksheet screen.

Enter **procalc** at the system prompt. A copyright information screen appears momentarily. Then Professional displays the worksheet screen, with the highlight in the upper left corner as in Figure 8.2.

The worksheet is divided into columns, which are designated by letters, and rows, which are numbered. Each rectangular space where a column and a row intersect on the worksheet is called a *cell*. When you start Professional, the highlight is on the cell at the intersection of

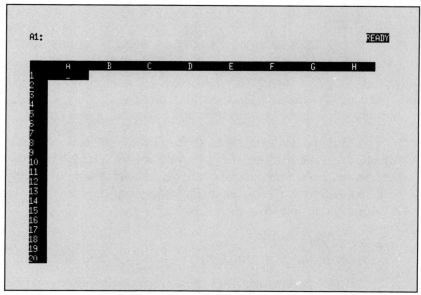

Figure 8.2: *The SCO Professional worksheet screen*

column A and row 1. The *address,* or location, of this cell is therefore A1, and the cell is referred to as *cell A1* or just *A1.* The *cell address indicator* at the top left corner of the screen shows you where you are.

As you can tell by the *mode indicator,* in the top right corner of the screen, you are ready to begin building a worksheet.

2. Use / (a slash) to access the command menu.

To use any of the worksheet commands, enter / (a slash). The command menu appears on the line below the cell address indicator. Below the command menu line there is a message line. It either lists the options that the highlighted command will give you, or gives you an explanation of the command. In Figure 8.3, the options for the highlighted **Worksheet** command appear on the message line. Moving the highlight to other commands will show different options. Some commands, like **Copy,** do not have an options menu. Highlighting one of these commands brings up an explanation of the command in the line where the options usually are.

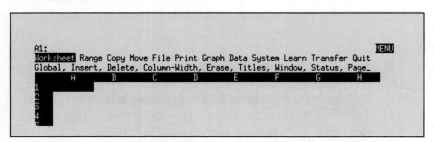

Figure 8.3: *The command menu line in the worksheet screen*

To move the highlight to different commands, use the → and ← keys. Press Return when the command you want is highlighted. If you know what a command does, you can choose it without highlighting it; just enter the first letter of the command, the way you would in Office Portfolio or Word for UNIX.

3. Move back from a lower-level command menu to the menu above it.

If you start at the main command menu and choose a command that displays a second menu of commands, and then continue the process until you are several levels down from the main menu, you can move back up to the the higher-level menus by choosing the **Quit** command in a menu (if there is one). If there is no **Quit** command, press the Escape key, and you will move to the next menu up.

*R*etrieving an Existing Worksheet File

Use the following procedure to display a previously saved worksheet file on the worksheet screen so you can view it, modify it, or make a graph for it.

1. Bring the blank worksheet screen into view.

If you have not already done so, use the **procalc** command from the system prompt to start Professional and display a blank worksheet screen.

2. List the available worksheet files.

Enter **/** (a slash) to display the command menu over the worksheet screen. To choose the **File Retrieve** command from the menu, enter **fr**. If there are any worksheet files in your working directory, Professional lists them on the options line below the menu. Worksheet files have the .wk1 extension.

Professional also displays a prompt on the menu line, asking you to enter the name of the file to retrieve. If you know the path and name of the worksheet file you want, you can enter it at the prompt and press Return. If you do not know the path and name of the file, use the next step to find and choose the file you want.

3. Choose the file you want to retrieve.

If you see the name of the file you want, move the highlight to it with the → and press Return. Don't try to choose the file by entering its first letter; that works with commands, but not with files. If the file is not in view, move the highlight to the right until all of the available files and directories have been displayed. If you still haven't seen the file you want, it might be inside one of the directories listed. Move the highlight to the correct directory name and press Return; then move the highlight through the files listed until you find the one you want, and press Return again.

When you choose a file, the worksheet screen appears with the file's data and labels in place.

4. Move around the worksheet.

To move to different cells on the worksheet, use the arrow keys or Control characters. For example, to move from A1 to A2, press ↓, or enter **Ctrl-J**. Table 8.3 shows different keystrokes to use to move around the worksheet.

Table 8.3: Keystrokes for Moving Around the Worksheet in SCO Professional

KEYSTROKE	HIGHLIGHT MOVEMENT
↓ *or* Ctrl-J	Down one cell
↑ *or* Ctrl-K	Up one cell
→ *or* Ctrl-L	To the right one cell
← *or* Ctrl-H	To the left one cell
PgDn *or* Ctrl-D	Down one screen
PgUp *or* Ctrl-U	Up one screen
Tab *or* Ctrl-N	To the right one screen
Shift-Tab *or* Ctrl-P	To the left one screen
Home	To cell A1
F5 *cell address*	To the specified cell

The highlight acts as your cursor as you move around in the worksheet. If you move the highlight off the screen, the worksheet scrolls in whichever direction is necessary, showing you the rest of the worksheet, which is too big to be shown on one screen. The worksheet can be much, much larger than the 8-column by 19-row window you see when you start Professional. You can build a worksheet with as many as 1024 columns and 8192 rows! Figure 8.4 shows the window you see on the screen, and the rest of the worksheet beyond it.

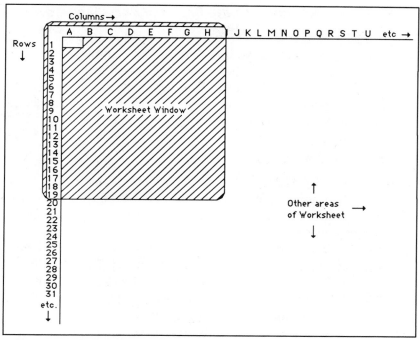

Figure 8.4: *Your window on the worksheet*

Planning and Labeling Your Worksheet

You will want to plan what kind of data you will need on the spreadsheet carefully. While such a vast topic as spreadsheet design is beyond this book's scope, general good practice is to keep things as simple as you can within the constraints of the task to be done. It may help to sketch out what you will eventually want the worksheet to produce beforehand.

When you have planned out how many columns and rows you need to start building your worksheet, you can enter labels in the first column and in the top row. You may wish to title the worksheet; in this case use the row below the title row. Whether you are entering a label, a value, or a formula in a cell, what you enter appears in the cell and next to the cell address indicator at the top of the screen. Use the following procedure to enter these labels, and then to "freeze" them, so that you can still see them if you scroll to different areas of the worksheet.

1. Move the cursor to the first row to be labeled.

Use the arrow keys to move the highlight to the cell in column A where you want to put your first label. For example, if you are building an annual expense report, you might want to have labels for the months of the year running down the A column, starting on row 5. This leaves you 4 rows at the top of the worksheet for a worksheet title and your column labels.

2. Enter the first label.

Type in the label for the row. If the label begins with text, just type it in. For example, type **Jan-91** to label a row for the first month of 1991. When you press Return, the label appears in the highlighted cell.

If you want to enter a label that starts with a number, first type a label prefix character. For example, if you want to use the label 1-91 you need to enter **'1-91** and press the Return key. This is so that Professional does not calculate the numbers as a formula, and put **– 90** (one minus 91) in the cell, or **(90.00)** (meaning a negative $90 balance) if you are dealing with monetary values.

Notice that the mode indicator at the upper-right corner of the screen says **LABEL** when you are entering a label, and **VALUE** if you are entering numbers or formulas in the cell.

The apostrophe indicates a left-justified label, one aligned on the left-hand side of the cell. If you want to right-justify a label you can use " (a double-quote) as a label prefix; to center a label, prefix it with the ^ (a caret) symbol.

3. Enter the other labels.

Enter all of the row labels in the same column. When you enter column labels, enter them all in the same row. If you enter a column label that is longer than the column width, and then enter another label in the next column to the right, the second label will cover the end of the first. Don't worry about this, as long as the column is wide enough to show the values you eventually want to put in it. If you ever need to see the full label for the column, you can move the highlight to it; it will appear by the cell address indicator at the top of the screen.

4. Use F2 *to edit previously entered labels.*

If you create a label with a mistake in it, and then move on to another cell, you can still fix the error. Move the highlight back to the cell with the faulty label, then press the **F2** key to go into Edit mode. The mode indicator changes to **EDIT** and the editing cursor appears at the end of the label, by the cell address indicator at the top of your screen. Backspace over the mistaken characters or delete them with the Delete key, and then reenter the correct label.

5. Freeze the labels on a large worksheet.

If you build a worksheet that fills more than one screen, you will notice that the row labels disappear from view if you move to the right on the worksheet, and the column labels disappear if you move down. To prevent this, move the cursor to the first *data* cell, to the right of the row labels and just below the column labels. For example, if your column labels are in row 5, and your row labels are in column A, move the highlight to cell B6. Then enter **/wt** to get into the command menu and choose the **Worksheet Titles** command. This will tell Professional to keep your label columns and rows in place as you scroll up, down, or sideways in the worksheet.

Entering Values and Formulas

After entering labels for the rows and columns of your worksheet, you can start filling in values and formulas in the cells that call for these. For example, in an annual expenses report, you might enter the amounts paid out each month for a given item, and then, in a row below the monthly amounts, enter a simple formula to add up the monthly expenses and display the annual total. Use the following procedure to enter the values and formulas you need to build your worksheet.

1. Format the values you want to enter.

If you are going to be entering values that all have the same format, such as currency, you can make a global setting for the worksheet, so all the numbers will be aligned correctly in the columns, and dollar signs will appear where appropriate. Enter **/w** to choose the

Worksheet command in the main menu, then enter **g** to choose **Global**, and **f** to choose **Format** . When the Format menu appears, choose the type of format you want for your values.

If you choose **Currency**, you see a prompt for the number of decimal places. Press the Return key to accept the default, which is 2. All values you enter on the worksheet will now be displayed in dollars and cents.

If you choose other formats, the values will be displayed as specified. You can use date format, scientific notation, or percentages; you can even hide the values from view.

2. Move to a cell and enter a value.

Use the arrow keys or Control characters to move to a cell in the worksheet in which you wish to enter a value. To enter a value, just enter it in numbers. Do not enter a comma in a number—for example, you should enter 4352 instead of 4,352. You do not have to enter dollar signs at the beginning of currency values, either. You should, however, enter a dot for a decimal value—enter 4352.26 rather than 435226.

3. Move to a cell and enter a formula.

A formula can be anything from a simple arithmetical expression, like **44-B6** (the value in cell B6 subtracted from 44), to complex worksheet mathematics expressions with automated macros, built-in functions, and sequential operations. Information on using advanced formulas is included in your SCO Professional documentation.

If you want to begin a formula with a cell address, you must put a mathematical operator before the first column letter. For example, Professional recognizes **+B6-44** as formula, but **B6-44** would be considered a label, because it starts with a letter.

You can use the following operators to do math in formulas:

Operator	Meaning
+	Addition
−	Subtraction
*	Multiplication
/	Division
^	Exponentiation

4. Point to a cell to enter it in a formula.

If you are entering a formula in a cell, you can use the point function to specify another cell as part of the formula. For example, if you are in cell B7 and you want to enter **+B6-44** as your formula, first enter the **+** sign, then move the highlight up to the B6 cell. Then enter **-44** and press Return. The formula appears next to the cell address indicator, and the result of the formula appears in the B7 cell on the worksheet. To use the above example, if cell B6 contains the value 50 and you enter the formula **+B6-44** for cell B7, the result, 6, appears in cell B7 when you press Return.

5. Define ranges for a function in a formula.

Functions are shorthand designations for particular kinds of calculations you might want to perform on a number of cells. If you use a function as part of a formula for a cell, and the function calls for values from a number of connected cells, you can select all these cells together as a *range* and the function will act on all of them.

Ranges are consecutive cells in a row or a column, or a rectangular block of cells in several rows and several columns. Note that an irregular shaped range cannot be achieved, as shown in Figure 8.5.

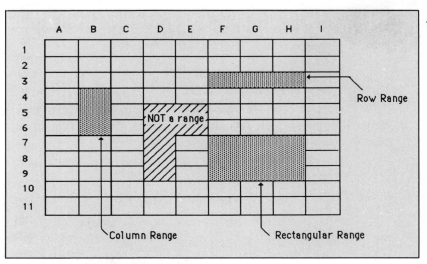

Figure 8.5: *Types of ranges you can select*

If you want to put the sum of the values in cells B4, B5, and B6 in cell B7, you can enter @**SUM(** in cell B7. Then move the highlight to cell B4, enter **.** (a period) as an anchor, and move the highlight again, this time to cell B6. All three cells become highlighted. Enter **)** (a right parentheses) to complete the formula. It should now read @**SUM(B4..B6)** next to the cell address indicator at the top of your screen. Press Return, and the sum of the values in cells B4, B5, and B6 will appear in cell B7.

You can use this pointing and anchoring technique to highlight any of the types of ranges shown in Figure 8.5, and you can use these ranges in any command or function that calls for a range.

Displaying Your Worksheet Data in Graph Form

Once you have completed a worksheet, you can display all or part of the data in graph form. To create a graph from the data on a worksheet, use the following procedure.

1. Choose the type of graph you want to create.

Enter **/gt** to get to the command menu and choose **Graph Type**. This menu offers you your choice of a graph to create: Line, Bar, XY, Stack-Bar, or Pie. Choose the type that suits your data. For example, if your worksheet compares monthly expenses, you might choose a bar graph. After you have made a choice, Professional returns you to the Graph menu.

2. Select data ranges to be graphed.

Enter one or more of the letters **a, b, c, d, e,** or **f** and specify a range of data for each. The ranges will depend on the type of data you want to graph. Make sure the ranges relate reasonably to each other, so the graph displays your information clearly and meaningfully.

3. Add a legend and titles to the graph.

Use the command **/gol (Graph Options Legend)** to create a legend for your graph, giving each range a name that reflects the source of the data. The names can be up to 19 characters long. Enter **/got (Graphs Options Titles)** to specify a first and second title for the entire graph, and titles for the X-axis and Y-axis. These titles are limited in length only by the size of the graph.

4. Add labels to the X axis of the graph.

You can take the column or row labels from your worksheet to provide appropriate labels. If these labels are too long to fit on the X axis of the graph, you can create short versions of the labels in a range that is to one side of your worksheet, and then enter **/gx (Graph X)** and specify that range as the x-axis label. For example, if you are creating a bar graph, enter short labels in an unused range for the rows or columns that contain data to be represented by the bars. Then use **/gx** to select that range. These labels will appear along the X axis, under the appropriate bars.

5. View the graph when you have finished it.

Enter **/gv (Graph View)** to display the graph on your screen. Check the graph to make sure the correct information is shown, and that it is visually clear. If there are elements of the graph that are not clear, you may want to adjust the labels, change the scale, or add color to maximize the graph's visual impact. A sample bar graph is shown in Figure 8.6. It shows its information clearly and simply.

For more information on these and other graph options, see the SCO Professional documentation.

Getting Help While Using Professional

If you have difficulty understanding a command or some aspect of modifying your worksheet, you can always read the online Help screen for information and brief instructions.

1. Press F1 to see a pop-up Help message.

If you need help on a specific command or element of the worksheet, move the highlight to the command or element. Then, before you do anything else, press the **F1** key. If your keyboard has no Function keys, enter **Ctrl-F-1** (hold down the Control key, press **f**, then press **1**). A small pop-up Help screen appears, explaining the current command or worksheet element. Read the screen, and if you do not need more help, press Return to return to your work.

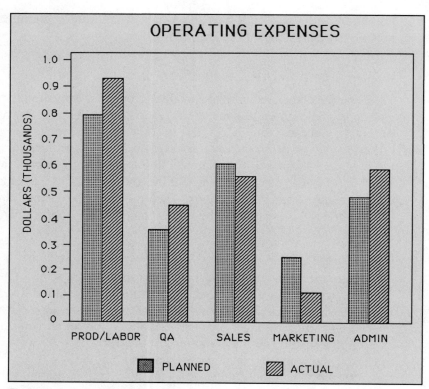

Figure 8.6: *A simple worksheet graph*

2. Use **F1** *again to see a full Help screen.*

If you need more help than the pop-up screen gives, press **F1** again. A full-size Help screen appears, with a menu at the top.

If there is more than one page of Help text on your topic, and you need to read the next page, press Return or enter **c** to continue reading about your topic.

3. Use the Index command to choose other Help topics.

If you do not find the information you need in the Help screens on your topic, enter **i** to see an index of all available Help topics. Move the highlight to the topic you want to see and press Return to see the Help information on that topic.

4. Enter h *if you have problems using the help screens.*

For explanations of the help screens, index, and help menu, enter **h** to choose the Help command from the menu.

5. *Return to your work with* Quit.

When you have finished using the on-line help screens, enter **q** to choose Quit and return to your work.

Saving Your Worksheet

Use the following procedure to save a worksheet file you have created. You should save a worksheet often as you are building it, so that your work will not be lost. If you want to keep older versions as you experiment with new data or formats, use the **Backup** option described in step 3.

1. Save your worksheet.

Enter **/fs** to choose the **File Save** command. A prompt appears, asking you to enter a name for a worksheet you have not saved before or to confirm the same worksheet name if you have saved it previously.

2. Name the file if it is new, or accept the name given.

If you have not named the file yet, enter a file name of 10 characters or less and press the Return key. If you want to protect the file with a password, enter a space and **p** after the file name, before you press Return.

If you have named the file already, or if you have retrieved a named file, the path and file name appear at the file name prompt. Press Return to confirm the old name of the file.

3. Decide if you want to keep an old version as a backup.

If you save a file that has been saved before, or that you have retrieved and modified, Professional presents you with three choices: you can **Cancel** the save command, **Replace** the old file, or choose the

Backup option. If you choose **Backup**, UNIX places the old version of the file in a /probackup directory in the working directory, and then saves the new version.

*P*rinting a Worksheet

Printing a worksheet as it appears on the screen is a three-part process:

- Choosing a range of data to print
- Selecting a printer or printing configuration
- Starting the printing process

Use the following procedure to print a section of a simple worksheet.

1. Save your worksheet file before printing.

Enter **/fs (File Save)** as described above. This is always a good precaution, in case there is a problem during the formatting or printing process.

2. Check the printer to make sure it is ready.

Make sure there is paper in the printer, and that it is turned on and ready to go. If you have fan-fold paper, make sure the top of the first page is lined up with the print head.

3. Choose the part of the worksheet you want to print.

If you're in the worksheet you want to print, enter **/ppr** to choose **Print, Printer,** and **Range**. Professional asks you to enter the range you want to print. You can either enter the range as requested, or select a range by entering . (a period) in the current highlighted cell, moving the highlight to the last cell in the range you want to print, and pressing Return. If you are printing a small part of a worksheet, you might be able to include the row and column labels in the range so they are printed on the same page. When you press Return after choosing the range you want to print, the Printer menu appears again.

4. Enhance your
printout's appearance, or print formulas.

From the Printer menu, enter **o** to choose the **Options** command. With **Options**, you can make headers and footers, set margins, choose rows and columns with labels as borders, enter printer setup strings, specify page length, and print the underlying formulas that create the values in the cells. There are default settings for many of these options; you can alter the default settings, and then later clear the new settings with **/ppc (Print Printer Clear)** and return to the defaults if you like.

5. Select a printer or printing configuration.

If you have a number of printers on your UNIX system, or if your printer has a number of configurations for different printing situations, you need to select the printer or printing configuration that is best for printing Professional worksheets.

From the Printer menu, enter **s** to choose **Select**. A list of printers and printing configurations is displayed; a description of the highlighted choice appears above the list. Use the arrow keys to highlight the choice you need; if you cannot tell which choice is best for printing Professional worksheets, ask your system administrator. When you press the Return key to select a printer or printing method, the Printer menu reappears.

6. Spool the selected range for printing.

From the Printer menu, enter **g** to choose the **Go** command. Your specified range is spooled for printing. Note that the printer does not print it out yet. If you are familiar with printing in other spreadsheet applications, you may expect **Go** to start the printing process; in Professional, however, it does not. This gives you the opportunity to select additional ranges to print before printing actually starts. If you do not need to print other ranges, go on to step 8.

7. Select other ranges and add them to the print spool.

From the Printer menu, enter **r** to select **Range,** if you wish to print a second range. When you are returned to the Printer menu, type **g (Go)** to add the second range to the spool with the first. If you want to change any of the options for the second range, you can use c **(Clear)** and o **(Options)** to reset these values. Repeat this process for as many ranges as you want to print.

8. Use the Quit
command to send all spooled ranges to the printer.

When you have finished selecting ranges you want to print and have given the **Go** command for each one, enter **q** from the Printer menu to send all of the spooled ranges to the printer at once. The menu disappears and you return to Ready mode, with the high-light in your worksheet. Unlike the usual UNIX print procedure, no request ID message appears.

Now, notice: you do not send your worksheet to the printer with the **/Print** command, nor do you send it with the **/Print Printer** com-mand, nor do you even send it with the **/Print Printer Go** command. These are only set-up commands. You actually send jobs to the printer with the **/Print Printer Quit** command. (Aah, the topsy-turvy world of UNIX!)

Quitting Professional

When you have finished work on a worksheet, use the following procedure to leave the Professional application and return to the sys-tem prompt.

1. Choose /Quit from the main menu.

There are **Quit** commands in several Professional menus, but only the **/Quit** command in the main menu allows you to exit from the applica-tion. If you are somewhere in the menu hierarchy, use the Escape key or the **Quit** commands in the lower level menus in order to return to either Ready mode or to the main menu. When you are in Ready mode, enter **/q** to exit from Professional. The **Quit** menu appears, with three options.

2. Choose a Quit option.

Your options from **Quit** are to save the worksheet as it now stands, to exit from Professional without saving any of your latest changes to the worksheet, or to cancel the **Quit** command and return to the worksheet.

If you enter **y** for Yes, you exit directly to the system prompt, and *you lose unsaved changes to the worksheet.* This is useful if you have made an error in the worksheet which would be difficult to fix otherwise; but only if you have not saved since making the error.

If you enter **s** for **Save**, a prompt appears at the top of your screen, asking you to enter the name of the new file to save or to confirm the name of a previously-named file.

3. Name the file if it is new, or accept the name given.

If you have not named the file yet, enter a name of 10 characters or less and press the Return key. If you want to protect the file with a password, enter a space and **p** after the filename before you press Return. You will be prompted for a password in this case.

If you have named the file already, or retrieved a named file, the path and file name appear at the file name prompt. Press the Return key to accept the name of the file.

4. Replace the old file, or keep it as a backup.

If you save a file that has been saved before, or that you have retrieved and modified, Professional presents you with three choices; you can **Cancel** the save command, **Replace** the old file, or choose the **Backup** option, which places the old version of the file in a /probackup directory in the working directory, then saves the new version.

If you choose **Cancel** you return to the worksheet. If you choose **Replace** or **Backup** the file is saved and the system prompt appears.

Using FoxBASE +

FoxBASE + is a database management program available on UNIX. This section will define databases, and then briefly describe how to:

- Start FoxBASE +
- Use the database screen and database files
- Get help while using FoxBASE +

- Create, save, and print database files
- Exit FoxBASE+

The descriptions of these procedures will assume that you are using FoxBASE+ without a menu interface, giving commands from a "dot prompt." If your version of FoxBASE+ includes a menu interface, such as FoxCentral, you can follow the procedures as described, using the menus to select the commands that the procedures call for. For more information on the commands and procedures, see the documentation for FoxBASE+.

Working with a Database

A *database* is an ordered collection of information, organized into *records*. Each record has several *fields*. For example, if you make a simple database from the contents of a telephone book, you would set up the listing for each person as a record, and make fields for the record number, last name, first name, street address, and phone number. Information organized like this for Eli Dake might look like this:

Record Number: 1

Last name: Dake

First name: Eli

Street address: 109 Calvin Place

Phone number: 423-7532

Typically, a database will have more than four fields in each record, and some of the fields might be much more extensive than those shown. But no matter how complex a database is, the basic structural units are records and fields. On the database screen, a record appears as a row of information, like this:

Record	LNAME	FNAME	STR_ADDR	PHONE
1	Dake	Eli	109 Calvin Pl	423-7532

If a number of records are displayed, all the data for a given field is therefore shown in a column down the screen.

You can use a database to organize and store any collection of information you want. You can add to or modify records, add new records, and delete old ones. You can sort the records in many ways, creating different ordered lists to suit your needs in different situations. You can *query* (search) the database for specific types of information, and you can create indexes for your database files, to make searches for information easier and less time-consuming. You can create reports, using specific data in specific fields. You can print specific records, specific fields from specific records, or reports you have formatted. If your database contains addresses, for instance, you could format and print address labels.

*S*tarting FoxBASE +

To start FoxBASE + and use the database files that are available to you, use the following two steps.

1. Move to your database file directory.

All of the database files you need for any given project should be in the same directory. Use **cd** *pathname* to move to that directory. If no database files exist yet, move to a directory where you can keep all the database files you create. Use **mkdir** if you need to make a new directory for your database files. (For help with these commands, see Chapter 4.)

2. Enter **foxplus** *to start FoxBASE +.*

The database screen appears, with its copyright information displayed in the main part of the window, as shown in Figure 8.7.

The copyright information will disappear as soon as you enter any command that displays something. The label "Command Line" in the reverse-video bar across the bottom of the screen refers to the blank area directly above it, where you enter commands next to the dot prompt. You will see your cursor at the beginning of the command line, one space to the right of the dot prompt. Whenever you see the cursor there, you can enter a command. You can enter commands in uppercase (capital) letters, as they are shown in the text, or in lowercase letters. The remainder of that reverse-video bar is called the *status bar,* which tells you what mode

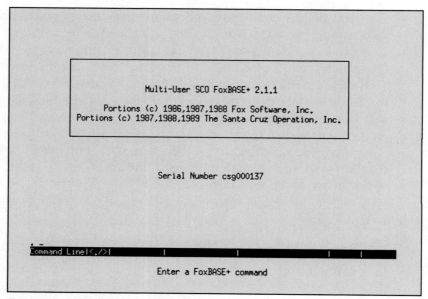

Figure 8.7: *The FoxBASE + database screen*

you're in and reports what you have done. Beneath the status bar is an information line, which tells you what you can do in the current screen or field.

Creating a Database

The following procedure explains the basic steps for creating a simple address-book database. Creating a database involves opening a database file, formatting its fields, and then entering your records.

1. Enter create filename *to start making a database.*

At the dot prompt, enter

create *filename*

The *filename* should be ten characters long or less and indicate what the database contains. For example, if I want to create a list of the addresses of my most important publishing contacts, I might enter

create pubaddr

FoxBASE+ displays a form for setting up the structure of your database, field by field, shown in Figure 8.8.

Near the top of the screen there is a help window that tells you how to move the cursor, how to enter and delete things in the form, and how to do a few other key functions. The ^ (caret) symbols in this window stand for the Control key: to insert a field, for instance, you would type **Ctrl-N**.

In the middle of the screen there are four highlighted blank spaces, for specifying a new field's name, type, width, and decimal placement. The cursor appears in the first blank space.

At the bottom of the screen are two information lines. The upper one tells you what to do in the blank where the cursor is, and the lower one lists restrictions on what you can do there.

2. Specify the formats for your first field.

All you have to do is fill in the blanks, right? But you'll need to do a little planning before you fill them in. For example, if I want my address list to look like this:

LNAME	FNAME	STR_ADDR	CITY	STA	ZIP
Snood	Phillis	900 Yurok St	Barstow	CA	90000

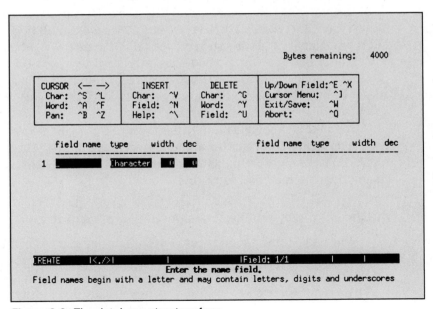

Figure 8.8: *The database structure form*

and I want all 6 fields to fit on my terminal's screen at one time, the widths of my fields have to add up to less than 64 characters or vertical positions on the screen. My first field is the last name field. I'll call it **lname** for short, and press the Return key to move on to the type blank, which already has **Character** in it. Since this field is going to have characters in it, I can just press Return and go on to the width blank. Most last names have less than 15 characters, so I enter 15 and press the Return key. The **dec,** or decimal, blank only applies to fields of the numeric type, so FoxBASE+ skips it for this character-type field, and moves down to a new, second field.

If you make mistakes specifying things for your fields, backspace over them and enter them again, or use the cursor-movement and editing keys shown in the help window.

3. Specify the formats for your other fields.

Enter a field name, type, and width for each field. If you are going to enter currency amounts, or numbers that you will need to do math with, use the **Numeric** type and specify a decimal placement for the field. If you are going to enter dates in the field, select the **Date** type. If the field is going to be either true or false, select the **Logical** type. If you want to enter long text messages and keep them off the screen, use the **Memo** type. Otherwise, leave the type set to **Character** for all fields, as I did in my simple database structure, shown in Figure 8.9.

Notice that even my zip code field is a character-type field. Even though zip codes in the United States are always numbers, other countries use letters in their zip codes. It's better to leave the **Character** type specified for the field.

To make an abbreviated field name more clear, you may want to use the underline character for a space, as I did in the **STR_ADDR** field name. Spaces and other punctuation are not allowed in field names, so an underline is a good substitute.

4. Check, save, and exit the database structure.

When you think the fields are set up right, examine the settings carefully and imagine how the fields will look spread across the screen. Edit any of the fields that are not just the way you want them. If you press the Return key by mistake when you are done with the last

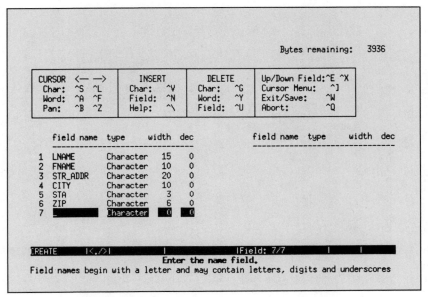

Figure 8.9: *A simple database structure*

field you want to enter, the blanks for another field will appear, as shown in Figure 8.9. Don't panic: press Return again to delete the extra field.

Enter **Ctrl-W** to save the structure you have made for your database and exit the database structure form. FoxBASE+ asks if you want to input data records now.

5. Enter your first record in the database.

Enter **y** to enter data for the first record in the database you are creating. The data entry screen looks like the one shown in Figure 8.10.

Now all you have to do is fill the blanks for all the fields. For example, to create a record for an imaginary publisher, Phillip Snood, I would fill in the blanks starting with his last name, then his first name, street address, city, state, and zip code. After completing the entry for each field, I press Return to move on to the next field. After I fill in all of the fields, the record would look like Figure 8.11.

If you make mistakes filling in the blanks, backspace over them and enter the correct data, or use the cursor movement and deletion keystrokes in the help window.

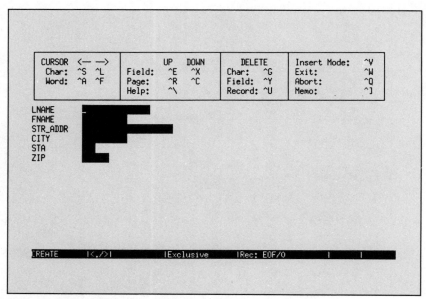

Figure 8.10: *A FoxBASE + data-entry screen*

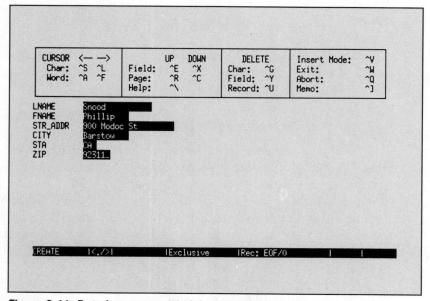

Figure 8.11: *Data for one record of the database*

When you have entered all the correct data for a record, use **Ctrl-C** or move the cursor to the end of the last field and press the Return key; the screen reopens for the next record.

6. Enter more records, then exit from the data entry form.

Data-entry is the least fun part of databases. Enter the data carefully, though, so you don't have to do it over. When you have filled all of the fields for the last record, enter **Ctrl-W** to exit from the form.

If you press the Return key instead of entering **Ctrl-W** at the end of your last record, you end up with a blank extra record at the end of your database. Enter **Ctrl-U** to mark the blank record for deletion, then enter **Ctrl-W** to exit. Enter **pack** at the dot prompt to complete the deleting process. (These commands are explained in more detail later.)

*M*anaging an Existing Database File

The following procedure describes how to access an existing database file. It tells how to list records, and how to sort, append, insert, edit, and delete them. You should already have started the FoxBASE+ program with the **foxplus** command at your UNIX system prompt.

1. List available database files.

Use the **DIR** command at the FoxBASE+ dot prompt to see what databases, if any, are available for use. **DIR** lists only those database files that can be used by FoxBASE+. All of these files have the .dbf extension. The listing tells the name of each database file, the numberof records in it, the date it was last modified, and its size in bytes.

2. Access a database file.

At the dot prompt, enter

use *filename*

and press Return. You do not have to enter the .dbf extension as part of the filename. The name of the file appears in the status line of the database screen.

For example, if my working directory contains a database file named pubaddr.dbf, I enter

use pubaddr

The PUBADDR file name appears in the status line.

3. List the records in your database.

At the dot prompt, enter

list *scope*

where *scope* indicates which records are to be listed. Table 8.4 explains different scope options you can use. Notice that the NEXT and REST scopes both include the current record.

Table 8.4: Scope options in FoxBASE +

SCOPE	LISTS
ALL	All records in the database
NEXT *n*	The next *n* records, including the current one
RECORD *n*	Only record number *n*
REST	All of the records from the current one to the end of the database

For example, if I enter **list all** at the dot prompt, I see all six of the records in my database, as shown in Figure 8.12.

If I enter 2 and press Return, to make the second record the current one, then enter **list next 3** and press Return again, FoxBASE + displays the listing shown in Figure 8.13.

```
Record#  LNAME      FNAME    STR_ADR          CITY      STA ZIP
      1  Snood      Phillis  900 Yurok St     Barstow   CA  92311
      2  Sproung    George   122 Pear Ave     Jolon     CA  93928
      3  Queen      Dianne   2021 Hoopa St    Freedom   CA  95019
      4  Zummerman  Albert   29 West 21st St  Olema     CA  94950
      5  Youngfort  Dan      112 Weed St      Hayfork   CA  96041
      6  Bruchini   Rachael  5 Banjo St       Swanton   CA  95017
```

*Figure 8.12: A **list all** of the pubaddr database*

```
Record#  LNAME       FNAME     STR_ADR          CITY      STA ZIP
      2  Sprung      George    122 Pear Ave     Jolon     CA  93928
      3  Queen       Dianne    2021 Hoopa St    Freedom   CA  95019
      4  Zummerman   Albert    29 West 21st St  Olema     CA  94950
```

Figure 8.13: Listing the next three records

Other arguments can also be added to the **LIST** command. If I want to list only the information in the LNAME and CITY fields, for instance, I can enter

> **list all lname, city**

4. Arrange your records in alphabetical order.

If you want to create a database file that contains all your records in alphabetical order, enter

> **sort to** *filename* **on** *field*

where *filename* is the name of a new database file you are creating, and *field* is the field you want to base the sorting on. For example, if I want my address list to be arranged so that people's last names are in alphabetical order, I can enter

> **sort to pubaddrlst on lname**

and my records are alphabetized in the pubaddrlst file. If I enter **use pubaddrlst** to access the new file, then enter **list all**, the records are listed as shown in Figure 8.14.

```
Record#  LNAME       FNAME     STR_ADR          CITY      STA ZIP
      1  Bruchini    Rachael   5 Banjo St       Swanton   CA  95017
      2  Queen       Dianne    2021 Hoopa St    Freedom   CA  95019
      3  Snood       Phillis   900 Yurok St     Barstow   CA  92311
      4  Sprung      George    122 Pear Ave     Jolon     CA  93928
      5  Youngfort   Dan       112 Weed St      Hayfork   CA  96041
      6  Zummerman   Albert    29 West 21st St  Olema     CA  94950
```

Figure 8.14: The new, sorted pubaddlst database

This new sorted file is much easier to use than the original, so it often becomes the file you work with. It's advisable, however, to be careful to remember which database has the most current information in it, and to delete out-of-date ones promptly.

5. Add records to the database.

From the dot prompt, use the **APPEND** command to add a record to the end of the existing database. If the database is sorted and you want to add a record in the correct order, first enter the number of the record that will follow the new record, then use the **INSERT BEFORE** command to add the new record in the correct place.

Both of the above commands open the data entry form as shown back in Figure 8.10. Follow the procedure in the "Creating a Database" section to enter the data for your new record.

6. Modify specific records and fields.

If you have to make changes or additions to the data in specific records and fields, you can use the **EDIT** command, specifying a scope as shown back in Table 8.4, and listing the fields you want to edit in the specified records, as follows:

edit *scope* **fields** *list*

For instance, if I want to correct a mistaken zip code in the Queen record of my pubaddrs database, I can enter the command

edit record 2 fields zip

and the data entry form opens with the cursor in the zip field of the Queen record.

7. Delete old records.

If a record is outdated or no longer useful, mark it for deletion, and then erase it from the database file. At the dot prompt, enter

delete *scope*

specifying a record or records with the scope argument as described in Table 8.4. If you list your database after using this command, it will still appear in the list, but with * (an asterisk) after the record number. If you then enter **pack** at the dot prompt, the record is removed from the database permanently. It is very important to list the files and check the ones you have marked for deletion before using the **PACK** command. There is no way to recover a record that has been deleted with **PACK**.

How to Get Help While Using FoxBASE +

You can see on-line help at any time by using the following procedure. The cursor should be next to the dot prompt to start. If the cursor is in a field, use the Escape key or the exit keystrokes to return the cursor to the dot prompt.

1. Enter help at the dot prompt.

When you press Return after entering **help**, the Help Topic index fills the screen. The highlight is on the first topic, <ALIAS>.

2. Select a topic from the Help Topics list.

Look through the list to find the topic you need help with. Move the highlight to the topic, either by using the arrow keys or by entering the first two or three letters of the topic. For example, if you want help with the **CREATE** command, find it in the list, then move the highlight to it either by using the → and ↓ keys, or by entering **cr**. If you enter letters to move the highlight, they appear in the status bar, as shown in Figure 8.15.

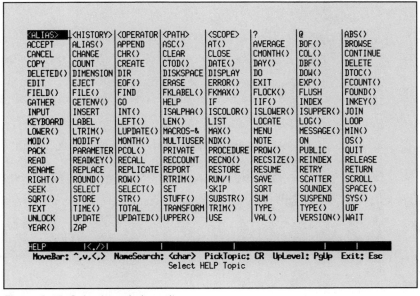

```
<ALIAS>      <HISTORY>  <OPERATOR  <PATH>      <SCOPE>    ?           @           ABS()
ACCEPT       ALIAS()    APPEND     ASC()       AT()       AVERAGE     BOF()       BROWSE
CANCEL       CHANGE     CHR()      CLEAR       CLOSE      CMONTH()    COL()       CONTINUE
COPY         COUNT      CREATE     CTOD()      DATE()     DAY()       DBF()       DELETE
DELETED()    DIMENSION  DIR        DISKSPACE   DISPLAY    DO          DOW()       DTOC()
EDIT         EJECT      EOF()      ERASE       ERROR()    EXIT        EXP()       FCOUNT()
FIELD()      FILE()     FIND       FKLABEL()   FKMAX()    FLOCK()     FLUSH       FOUND()
GATHER       GETENV()   GO         HELP        IF         IIF()       INDEX       INKEY()
INPUT        INSERT     INT()      ISALPHA()   ISCOLOR()  ISLOWER()   ISUPPER()   JOIN
KEYBOARD     LABEL      LEFT()     LEN()       LIST       LOCATE      LOG()       LOOP
LOWER()      LTRIM()    LUPDATE()  MACROS-&    MAX()      MENU        MESSAGE()   MIN()
MOD()        MODIFY     MONTH()    MULTIUSER   NDX()      NOTE        ON          OS()
PACK         PARAMETER  PCOL()     PRIVATE     PROCEDURE  PROW()      PUBLIC      QUIT
READ         READKEY()  RECALL     RECCOUNT    RECNO()    RECSIZE()   REINDEX     RELEASE
RENAME       REPLACE    REPLICATE  REPORT      RESTORE    RESUME      RETRY       RETURN
RIGHT()      ROUND()    ROW()      RTRIM()     RUN/!      SAVE        SCATTER     SCROLL
SEEK         SELECT     SELECT()   SET         SKIP       SORT        SOUNDEX     SPACE()
SQRT()       STORE      STR()      STUFF()     SUBSTR()   SUM         SUSPEND     SYS()
TEXT         TIME()     TOTAL      TRANSFORM   TRIM()     TYPE        TYPE()      UDF
UNLOCK       UPDATE     UPDATED()  UPPER()     USE        VAL()       VERSION()   WAIT
YEAR()       ZAP

HELP           |<,/>|        |           |         |           |           |
    MoveBar: ^,v,<,>   NameSearch: <char>   PickTopic: CR   UpLevel: PgUp   Exit: Esc
                              Select HELP Topic
```

Figure 8.15: *Selecting a help topic*

If you make a mistake entering the letters, press the Backspace key once to erase all the letters, and try again. When the topic you need help on is highlighted, press Return. A full-screen help message appears.

3. Read the help message on your topic.

If there is more than one page of help information, press any key to read the following pages. When you reach the end of a message, related subtopics (if there are any) are listed at the bottom of the screen, with the highlight on the first subtopic. To choose one of the others, move the highlight as before by pressing the arrow keys or entering the first letter of the subtopic you want.

When you have read as much of the topic or subtopic as you need, press the Escape key to return to the command line and continue work.

Printing Specified Data from the Database

There are different methods of sending data to the printer while using FoxBASE +, depending on what type of material you want to print. Three of them follow; use the one that applies to your table most closely, or see your FoxBASE + documentation for more information.

1. Print a formatted report based on numerous records.

If you want to use the information in many records to make a point, you should format the information so your point is clear. Enter

create report

at the dot prompt, and FoxBASE + gives you a report format screen which presents you with all the options you need to format your report. The result of this command is a format file, based on the data in the database currently in use. To send the report to the printer, enter

report form *filename* **to print**

where *filename* is the format file you have created. A request ID message appears.

2. Print mailing labels based on address records.

If the database file currently in use is one containing addresses, you can create mailing labels based on these addresses. The **CREATE LABEL** command allows you to make a standard mailing label format file based on the information in the current database. Then enter

label form *filename* to print

to designate the format file you have created for printing. The file does not actually go to the UNIX print spooler until you enter

set print off

at which point a request ID message appears.

3. Send specific records to the printer.

If you want to print out only a few records of the database, and if they will print in a reasonably clear format as they appear on the screen, you can enter

list *scope* to print

where *scope* specifies the records to be printed. The records are then designated for printing, but they do not actually go to the UNIX print spooler until you enter

set print off

A request ID message appears when the reports have gone to the spooler. Be aware, when using this method of printing, that wide records may run off the edge of the printed page, even if they wrap on the screen.

You can use the **TO PRINT** clause with many list and display commands as well. Use these commands to print information about your database files. For example, entering

list structure to print

will print out the structure of the current database.

Saving Your Database Files and Exiting FoxBASE+

All your work is saved automatically when you exit FoxBASE+ with the **QUIT** command. This is very convenient and makes for a quick exit from the application, but you must be sure you do not leave the application by use of a shell escape, then forget to come back to FoxBASE+ to end your FoxBASE+ session properly. Attempting to logout without leaving FoxBASE+ first can result in a loss of unsaved data.

When you enter **quit**, a message appears, telling you that Fox-BASE+ has had a normal shutdown. Then your system prompt reappears.

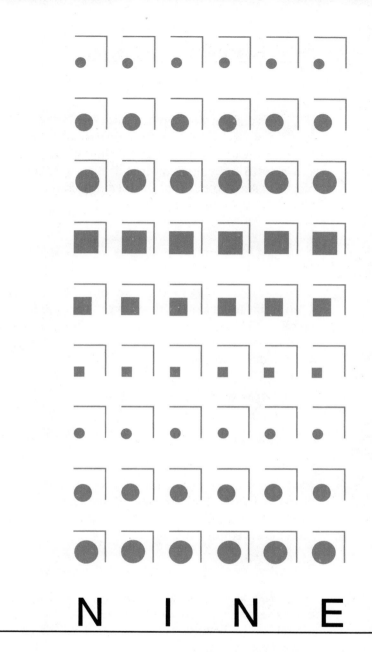

N I N E

**Advanced vi
Techniques**

This chapter develops your vi skills. It explains how to set up vi for editing, how to enter vi files, how to move around in the text, how to edit the text, how to search for things in the text and replace them, and how to use colon commands to move, copy, delete, and write blocks of text. Some of the basic editing commands you learned in the first chapter are repeated here.

Setting Up vi for Typing a Text File

If you are going to write a lot of text files using vi, you can make a setup file in your home directory that vi will look at every time you invoke it. This file will customize vi so it does some things automatically, every time you use it; that way, you won't have to reset custom settings over and over.

1. Change to your home directory.

Type

cd; lf -a

to list the files in your home directory. See if you have a file named **.exrc**; this is the setup file for vi. The name comes from UNIX's more primitive editing tool, *ex,* and *rc,* for *r*un-time *c*ommands. In other words, the .exrc file contains commands that are executed at the time you run the editor program.

2. Use vi to edit or create your .exrc file.

Whether you have a .exrc file in your home directory or not, enter the command **vi .exrc** in order to edit or create the file. If you are creating a new file, you'll see a blank screen with tildes running down the left side. If a file has been created for you or copied from somebody else's account, you may see a number of lines that begin with either **map** or **ab,** and there might be comment lines that begin with quotes, like this:

"Delete text marked a to b to buffer a:
map ;d :aa d a^M

"Yank text marked a to b to buffer a:
map ;y :aa ya a^M

These lines set up shortcuts for editing in vi. The two examples shown let you delete and yank blocks of text quickly. If your system has these shortcuts, ask an experienced user to show you how they can save you time.

3. Find the line for setting parameters.

If you are editing an old .exrc file, find the line that lets you set things up for your work in vi. (If you are creating a new .exrc file, go on to the next step.) It should start with **set** and contain some odd short words and equations. There may be a comment line preceding it. For example, my set-up line looks like this:

"Set these options:
set wm=20 dir=/y/tmp noic

These settings may be different than yours. The first one, **wm**, is the setting for your right margin (or *wrapm*argin). The second one is the directory where vi files are saved temporarily while you work on them. The last one stands for *no i*gnore *c*ase, and it means that vi will pay attention to whether the letters I specify for a search are uppercase or lowercase. I can search for "Big Apple," for instance, and vi will skip over *oranges, small apples,* and *big apple,* returning only the occurrences of *Big Apple* in the text.

4. Set your wrap margin to 20 spaces.

If you have a set line in your .exrc file, just add **wm = 20** to it. If there is no line starting with **set**, or if you are just starting a .exrc file, enter the following line:

set wm = 20

Make sure there is a space between **set** and **wm = 20** and that there are no spaces in the equation **wm = 20**. If you have a set line with other settings, you can add the **wm = 20** anywhere among them or at the end of the line, but make sure there is a space before and after the equation, to separate it from the other settings.

The **wm = 20** command sets the right margin, where words wrap to the next line, at 20 spaces. This is a pretty wide right margin, but there's a good reason for it. You often need some slack there. For instance, if you write a mail message and somebody forwards your message, it gets indented a bunch of spaces. If your message is so inspiring or controversial that it gets forwarded twice, it gets indented twice. If your double-indented message is wide, it goes off the right edge of the screen, and wraps in a peculiar way. It can come out of somebody's electronic mailbox looking like this:

> **About that message I got from tomc;**
> **you know, the one with the long lines:**
> > **From tomc Sun Jun 11 16:41 1991**
> > **To: dianew**
> > **Subject: Longevity**
> > **Date: Sun Jun 11 16:34:14 1991**
>
> > **This message may be a bit hard to foll**
> **ow because**
> > **the lines overflowed. The klutz who se**
> **nt it**
> > **blew it by writing long lines instead of**
> **setting**
> > **the right margin at 20.**

Nobody wants to read a message like that. Text can be indented for formatting reasons, too. If you set your wrap margin to 20 spaces in your .exrc file, you never have to worry about these problems, and your text wraps neatly and automatically every time you start vi.

Opening a vi File

There are a number of ways to use the **vi** command to open a file, depending on where you want to be in the file when the text appears on your screen. Before you can open a file and do all the editing described in the rest of this chapter, though, you need a file to experiment with.

If you have a long mail message or a text file of any kind, you can make a copy of it with **cp *filename* sample.text** command. This creates a copy of *filename* called sample.text, which you can work on, change, and make mistakes on without changing your original file. If you don't have any text files, just enter **vi sample.text** and type in the sample file shown in Figure 9.1.

```
              Vegetables
              Once I knew a girl who just loved vegetables. You
didn't dare leave this little bunny alone with a relish tray
or it would be instantly deflowered of its cauliflowerlets
and stripped clean of its carrot strips.
              But this girl is in the minority. For cold scientific
proof, do this: On one side of a plate, put a stack of
marinated string beans; on the other side, put a heap of
smoked oysters. Then observe carefully which gets left. You
needn't even be that fancy. A can of salted peanuts will win
over the string beans, hands down, every time.
              Facts must be faced. Vegetables simply don't taste
as good as most other things do. And there isn't a single
vegetable, hot or cold, that stands on its own two feet the
way a ripe peach does, or a strawberry. Even sweet corn
needs butter and salt. It is interesting to note that
vegetables beginning with A are the most self-sufficient:
artichokes, asparagus, and avocados, which have really
slithered out of the fruit kingdom by this time into the
vegetable kingdom, no matter what the botanists say.  But
the farther down the alphabet you go, through rutabagas,
spinach, and turnips, the more hopeless they become, given
all the butter and salt you've got.
              Actually, the food experts know this, too, way down
deep.  You can tell they do, from the reliance they put on
adjectives whenever they bump into a vegetable.  "And with
it serve a big bowl of tiny, buttery, fresh-from-the-garden
beets!" they'll cry.  But they're still only beets, and
there's no need to get so excited about it.

              From "The I Hate to Cook Book" by Peg Bracken,
              Harcourt, Brace & World, Inc., N.Y., 1960.
```

Figure 9.1: *Sample text, excerpted from THE I HATE TO COOK BOOK by Peg Bracken. (Copyright © 1960,1988 by Peg Bracken.)*

When you have entered the text for your sample file, exit vi with the **ZZ** command, then use the **lf** command to list the files in your working directory, to make sure you have created a sample.text file. From the system prompt, you can use any of the following methods to get back into your vi file again.

Open a vi file at the end.

Use the syntax **vi + *filename*** to open your file at the end. If you want to add something at the end of your sample file, for instance, you could enter

vi + sample.text

The file opens, with the cursor on the last line of text. For example, if I open my sample.text file about vegetables with this command, I see the screen appearing in Figure 9.2.

```
   slithered out of the fruit kingdom by this time into the
   vegetable kingdom, no matter what the botanists say.  But
   the farther down the alphabet you go, through rutabagas,
   spinach, and turnips, the more hopeless they become, given
   all the butter and salt you've got.
         Actually, the food experts know this, too, way down
   deep.  You can tell they do, from the reliance they put on
   adjectives whenever they bump into a vegetable.  "And with
   it serve a big bowl of tiny, buttery, fresh-from-the-garden
   beets!" they'll cry.  But they're still only beets, and
   there's no need to get so excited about it.
   ~
   ~
   ~
   ~
   ~
   ~
   ~
   ~
   ~
   ~
   "sample.text" 30 lines, 1562 characters
```

Figure 9.2: *A vi file opened with the* **vi + *filename*** *command*

The last line of text appears in the middle of the screen, so you have room to write new text below it. The opening message appears at the bottom of the screen as usual, telling you the name of the file you have opened, and how many lines and characters it contains.

Open a vi file at a specific word.

If you know exactly what word you want to start working on in your sample file when you open it, use **vi + /text filename**, where **text** is a word or phrase in *filename* where you want the cursor to appear. For example, if I want to change the word *rutabagas* to *rhubarb* in my sample.text file, I can enter

    vi + /rutabagas sample.text

The file opens with the cursor at the beginning of the line that has "rutabagas" in it.

Open a vi file at a specific line.

If you are familiar with the numbers of the lines of text in your file and you know what line number you want to edit, enter

    vi +*n* filename

where *n* is the number of the line you want to edit. For example, if I want to open my sample file at line number 20, I can enter

vi +20 sample.text

and the file will open with the cursor at the beginning of that line.

To see for yourself that you are on the line you specified, you can enter the colon command **:set number** and the numbers will appear at the left margin of your text. To learn more about line numbers, see the "Editing in Escape Mode" section later in this chapter.

Moving Around in a vi File

This section tells how to move the cursor in all directions, by small increments and large ones. It also tells how to scroll through the text in a file to bring other parts of it into view. To use the commands explained, you must have a vi file open, such as sample.text, and you must be in escape mode. If you aren't sure whether you are in escape mode or not, press the Escape key to make sure.

Move forward and back one word at a time.

To move the cursor to the first letter of the next *w*ord in the text, press the **w** key. To move the cursor *b*ack to the first letter of the preceding word in the text, press the **b** key. For example, if I have the cursor on the first **l** of **little** in the second line of my sample.text file, it looks like this:

leave this little bunny alone with

If I enter **w** the cursor moves to the first letter of **bunny**. If I enter **b** the cursor moves to the first letter of **this**.

Move to the end of a word.

If the cursor is on any letter in a word, you can move it to the *e*nd by pressing the **e** key. For example, if I have the cursor at the beginning of the word **bunny**, I can move it to the **y** by pressing **e**.

Move forward, back, up, and down one space at a time.

When you press the l key you move the cursor forward one space or character. Pressing h moves the cursor back one space or character. If you press k the cursor moves up one line, and pressing j moves the cursor down one line.

Move to the beginning or the end of a line.

If the cursor is somewhere in the middle of a line and you want to go to the beginning of the line, press 0 (zero). To move the cursor to the end of the line, press $. For example, if I have my cursor in the middle of a line, it looks like this:

stack of marinated string beans; on the other side, put a

If I enter 0 the cursor moves to the s of **stack**, and if I enter $ the cursor moves to the a at the end of the line. Anyone can see the logic of the zero being the key to move you to the beginning of the line, but the dollar sign is a little more obscure: it is derived from the hidden vi symbol for the end of a line, which is also a dollar sign.

Move to a specific line in the file.

If you want to see the line numbers of your file, enter the colon command :set number. Then you can enter the *n*G command, where *n* is the number of the line you want to go to. For example, if I want to move to line number 28 of the sample.text file after using the :set number command to see the line numbers, I can enter the command 28G and the text will scroll to line 28, where the cursor appears under the first letter of the line, like this:

**25 Actually, the food experts know this, too, way down
26 deep. You can tell they do, from the reliance they put on
27 adjectives whenever they bump into a vegetable. And with
28 it serve a big bowl of tiny, buttery, fresh-from-the-garden**

The G command is useful for moving to the beginning of the file and the end of the file without even looking at the line numbers. If you just enter G with no number the cursor goes to the end of the file. Enter 1G to go to the beginning of the file.

Move to your previous location in the file.

If you do some editing in one part of a file, then move to another part and do some more editing, you can go back to the location of your previous work by entering ″ (two apostrophes) in escape mode. If, for example, I change some text somewhere in the middle of the file, move to the end of the file and begin editing, and then realize I made a mistake in the middle of the file, I can get back easily by entering ″. The text scrolls to the location of my previous edit, and the cursor appears on the first line of that edit.

Move the cursor up and down in the current screen.

If you are editing at the bottom of the screen and you want to get up to the top or to the middle of it, use the **H** or **M**, respectively. To get to the bottom of the screen, use **L**. The letters stand for *H*igh, *M*iddle, and *L*ow. The cursor appears at the beginning of a line in all three cases, as shown in Figure 9.3.

```
    But this girl is in the minority.  For cold
scientific proof, do this: on one side of a plate, put a
stack of marinated string beans; on the other side, put a
heap of smoked oysters.  Then observe carefully which gets
left.  You needn't even be that fancy.  A can of salted
peanuts will win over the string beans, hands down, every
time.
    Facts must be faced.  Vegetables simply don't taste
as good as most other things do.  And there isn't a single
vegetable, hot or cold, that stands on its own two feet the
way a ripe peach does, or a strawberry.  Even sweet corn
needs butter and salt.  It is interesting to note that
vegetables beginning with A are the most self-sufficient:
artichokes, asparagus, and avocados, which have really
slithered out of the fruit kingdom by this time into the
vegetable kingdom, no matter what the botanists say.  But
the farther down the alphabet you go, through rutabagas,
spinach, and turnips, the more hopeless they become, given
all the butter and salt you've got.
    Actually, the food experts know this, too, way down
deep.  You can tell they do, from the reliance they put on
adjectives whenever they bump into a vegetable.  "And with
it serve a big bowl of tiny, buttery, fresh-from-the-garden
```

Figure 9.3: **H**, **M**, *and* **L** *positions on the screen*

Scroll up and down a line at a time.

If your cursor is in the middle of the screen somewhere and you want to see a line of text that is just out of view off the top of the screen, enter **Ctrl-Y** and the screen will scroll up a single line; the text moves down one line, in other words. Use **Ctrl-E** to see the next line of text below the screen. These two commands save you from either moving the cursor up and down a lot, or scrolling by a large increment and losing the cursor off-screen. If there is a logical reason for using the **Y** and the **E**, *y*ou can bet it *e*scapes me.

Scroll up and down a half screenful.

If you are editing near the top of the screen and want to see a few more lines of text above what is visible, enter **Ctrl-U** to move your view *u*p a half screenful. If you are working near the bottom of the screen, use **Ctrl-D** to scroll *d*own a half screen.

These commands are most useful when you are doing small edits every few lines, so you want to keep part of the text on the screen in view as you scroll to see new text.

Scroll up and down a full screen.

If you want to move quickly to a whole new screen of text above what's visible, use **Ctrl-B** to scroll *b*ack. To scroll *f*orward a screen, enter **Ctrl-F**. Notice that one or two lines of the text from the previous screen still show after you scroll; this keeps the continuity of the text, so you'll never wonder if something is missing between the two screenfuls.

Refresh the screen with Ctrl-R or Ctrl-L.

If someone interrupts your vi session with mail, or the system sends you a message, your screen may look odd. If there is a glitch in the computer or the communication lines, sometimes odd characters appear on your screen, too (this tends to happen most when you are communicating with the computer by modem). There is a way to bring your uncluttered screen back. Just enter **Ctrl-R** to *r*efresh the screen. Some terminals require **Ctrl-L** instead. The odd characters or messages disappear, and the text is displayed as it should be. If things still don't look right, see if you can edit out the problem text. If not, see the Troubleshooting sections for Chapters 1 and 2.

Inputting Text

This section explains a variety of ways to go into insert mode; there is also a way to replace a character and return to escape mode. Some of the commands may be familiar to you if you have been working in vi already.

Insert text at your current position.

Use i whenever you want to insert text at the cursor. Most of the rest of the input commands discussed in this section just give you shortcuts to moving the cursor and using i. One of the simplest shortcuts is to enter I (capital i) so you can go into insert mode at the beginning of the current line.

Append text after the cursor or the current line.

If the cursor is on the last letter of a word, you can *a*ppend text after the word by using a to go into insert mode. Use A to append text at the end of the current line, no matter where the cursor is in it. For example, I can add to the following line of text by both methods:

vegetables beginning with A are the most self-sufficient:

If the cursor is on the **h** in **with**, as shown, I can enter a and add a space and more text, such as **the letter**. If I want to add text to the end of the line, I can enter A and the cursor will jump to the space following the colon, ready for me to list things like amaranth and alfalfa sprouts.

Open a new line for text.

If the cursor is in the middle of a number of lines of text, and you want to start a new line below the current one, enter o. The blank line *o*pens and the cursor moves down to the beginning of it. All subsequent text moves down a line to make room for the new line. To open a new line for text above the line where the cursor is, enter O.

Replace a letter and return to escape mode.

If you mistype a letter and want to correct it and go on to other editing without having to go in and out of insert mode, move the cursor to the incorrect letter, enter **r**, and then *r*eplace the incorrect letter with the correct one. After you enter the correct letter, vi returns you to escape mode. You can then move the cursor or enter another command without having to press the Escape key.

For example, if I notice that I have spelled the word "botanists" incorrectly in my sample.text file, so it reads **botonists**, I can put the cursor on the **o** in the middle of the word, enter **r**, and then enter **a**. Then I can immediately enter a cursor movement command or a scrolling command, without pressing the Escape key.

Change a word or a line of text.

If you want to replace a word with one or more words, put the cursor at the first letter of the word, enter **cw** to *c*hange the *w*ord, then enter the new text. It may look as though you are overwriting other text, but it reappears as soon as you press the Escape key at the end of your insertion. To *c*hange the *c*urrent line of text, enter **cc** and then enter the new line. It can be shorter or longer than the line you are replacing.

For example, if I put the cursor on the following line:

it serve a big bowl of tiny, buttery, fresh-from-the garden

I could then enter **cc** and then something like:

it serve a bunch of boiled

The sentence would then read

And with it serve a bunch of boiled beets!

There are other commands for changing text; a brief listing of them appears in the Commands Summary at the end of this chapter.

Editing in Escape Mode

This section explains a wide variety of editing functions that you can do in Escape mode. There are commands for deleting and moving text, and commands for undoing mistakes, including previous deletions. There is also a command for repeating the previous command, and a command for joining two lines together.

Delete text with x, dw, dd, and D.

Use **x** to delete the character where the cursor is. Use **dw** to *d*elete a *w*ord if the cursor is on the first character of it. Use **dd** to delete the line where the cursor is, and use **D** to delete from the cursor to the end of the current line. You can put numbers in front of the **x**, **dw**, and **dd** commands. For example, if you want to delete 3 characters, enter **3x**; to delete 3 words, enter **3dw**, and to delete 3 lines, enter **3dd**. You can put numbers in front of many other editing commands, too.

You can move text by deleting it, then immediately moving the cursor to the new position, then entering **p** or **P**, as described in step 3 of this section. Deleted text is stored in a temporary buffer, a special place in the computer's memory; anything you delete is stored in this buffer until you edit something else. That is why you have to place the deleted text immediately after deleting it.

Yank text you want to copy with yw and yy.

Yanking text means taking a copy of what's on the screen and putting it in the temporary buffer. Enter **yw** to *y*ank a *w*ord, enter **yy** to yank a line of text. You can put numbers in front of the yank commands so they'll act on multiple words and lines.

For example, consider the following line of text:

Facts must be faced. Vegetables simply don't taste

I can make a copy of the first sentence of this line by putting the curser at the beginning, as shown, then entering **4yw**. If I want to put the copy in a new place in the text, I have to move the cursor, then use the **p** or **P** commands, as described in the next step of this section. I have to do this before I do any other yanking, changing, or deleting, because those actions overwrite the temporary buffer where the sentence is stored.

Place yanked or deleted text with p and P.

After deleting or yanking text, if you immediately move the cursor to a new place in the text, you can use either **p** to *p*ut the text after the cursor, or **P** to put the text before the cursor. If you have deleted or yanked lines of text, the **p** (lowercase) puts the lines below the current line, and the **P** (uppercase) puts the lines above the current line.

For example, if I move the cursor to the end of my sample.text file after yanking the sentence mentioned in the last step, I can use **o** to open a new line, then tab in for a new paragraph, then press the Escape key and enter **p** to begin that paragraph with my yanked sentence, like this:

> **beets!" they'll cry. But they're still only beets, and there's no need to get so excited about it.**
>   **Facts must be faced. _**

Yank a line of text to copy it to a new place later.

If you want to make a copy of the current line now and put it somewhere else in the file later on, use **"ayy**. This puts a copy of the line into buffer a, where it will not be overwritten until you leave vi or write something else to that buffer. Buffer a is one of 26 buffers named a to z; you can yank things into any of them for later use. You can take the text out of buffer a and put copies of it into the file as many times as you want, using the **"ap** or **"aP** commands as described below.

To yank a number of lines into buffer a, put the number between the **a** and the **yy**. For example, to yank 3 lines of text (the current line and two lines below it) into buffer a, I enter **"a3yy**.

You can also yank text into those 25 other buffers, with names from b to z. Just substitute the letter of the buffer for the **a** in the command above.

Delete a line of text to move it to a new place later.

If you are deleting a line of text and want to save it to put in a different place later, such as adding it to a part of the file that you haven't written yet, put the cursor anywhere in the line and enter **"add**. This puts the deleted line into a buffer; it will not be overwritten or removed until you write something else to that buffer or exit from vi. You can put the text back into the file as many times as you want; the **"ap** and **"aP** commands described in the next step just make copies of what is in the a buffer and put them into your file.

To delete a number of lines and save them in buffer a, put the number between the **a** and the **dd**. For example, **"a2dd** deletes the current line and the one below it, and keeps them in buffer a.

As with yanking, you can delete lines into 26 buffers, with names from a to z. Just substitute the letter of the buffer for the **a** in the **"add** command.

Put yanked or deleted lines in the text.

After yanking or deleting lines into buffer a, you can do other editing. Then, when you are ready to use the text in buffer a, move the cursor to the place where you want to put the text. Use **"ap** to put the lines after the current line, and use **"aP** to put the lines above the current line.

Move yanked or deleted lines to a different vi file.

You can move lines of text to a different file if you first save the last changes to your current file with the **:w** command, then use the **:e** *filename* command, where *filename* is the name of the file you want to put the lines into. When you are in the file, move the cursor to the place where you want to put the lines in buffer a, then use the **"ap** or **"aP** command to put the lines in place, as described in the previous step.

You can then return to the previous file by entering **:w** and then using the **:e #** command. The pound sign stands for "previous file." For more information on colon commands such as **:w** and **:e**, see the "Colon Commands" section later in this chapter.

Yank or delete larger blocks of text using a mark.

If you want to yank or delete more than a few lines of text, you can use a mark so you don't have to count the lines. Just move the cursor to the first line you want to yank or delete, enter **ma** while in escape mode, then move the cursor to the last line you want to yank or delete. Then, if you want to yank the whole block of text, enter **y'a** and press the Return key. If you want to delete the block of text, enter **d'a** and press the Return key. This is a powerful technique. Be careful where you place the cursor when you enter the mark and when you enter the yank or delete command. And remember that **u** *un*does the last command, if you make a mistake.

Join short lines together with **J**.

If you have edited a couple of lines and made them much shorter, you can join them together by moving the cursor to the upper line and entering **J**. For example, if I edited the first two lines of the last paragraph of my sample.text file, I might have something like this:

The experts know this, too.
You can tell by how they rely on

If I put the cursor in the first line, as shown, and enter **J**, the second line moves up and joins itself to the top line, so I get this:

The experts know this, too. You can tell by how they rely on

The new line may be too long, like the one in the example, but you can usually fix this by entering a carriage return at the normal margin so the extra words move to the next line. On some systems there may be a formatting command for adjusting a whole paragraph at a time; ask your system administrator if such a command is available for vi on your system.

Repeat commands with the . *command.*

If you want to do the same command twice in different places, you can move the cursor after using the command the first time, then enter . (a period) in the new location to repeat the command. For example, if I wanted to shorten all the eight-space tabbed indents on the first lines of the paragraphs in the sample.text file, I could move the cursor to the indent of the first paragraph and enter **cw**, then enter five spaces, then press the Escape key. Then I could simply move the cursor to each of the other paragraph indents and enter . to repeat the command.

Undo editing you have done with **u** *or* **U**.

To undo the last text-altering command you entered, just get into escape mode and enter **u**. To undo all the last changes you have done to the current line, enter **U**.

Retrieve previous deletions with **"1p**.

If you delete something you didn't want to, then go on to do other editing, you can still bring back that mistakenly deleted text, as long as you haven't exited from vi yet. Just move the cursor to the space where the deleted text should begin, and enter "1p to retrieve the text. If you have made another deletion since the one you want to retrieve, the latest will appear when you use the "1p command. But you can still get the previously deleted text. Just enter . (a period) to repeat the retrieval command, and vi will dig deeper into the computer's memory and bring back the second-to-last text you deleted. You can keep entering periods until you have retrieved the last nine deletions.

Searching for Text

In most UNIX documentation, this is referred to as searching for strings. Strings are simply groups of characters. Since you will probably be working with text in your vi files, I'm going to describe the searches in terms of text. The search function is very good in vi; I imagine this is true because the programmers who developed vi tended to lose things in their files a lot.

Search forward and backward through a file.

If the cursor is at the beginning of a file, you can search forward through the file for text with the **/text** command, where **text** is the word, phrase, or number you are looking for. Note that the **/** appears at the bottom of the page, followed by the text you specify. For example, if I have the cursor at the beginning of my sample.text file, I can enter **/is** and press the Return key, and the cursor goes to the first occurrence of the two letters **is**, which is in the word **this**, as shown in Figure 9.4.

To search backwards from the end of a file, use the ?*text* command, instead of /*text*.

Continue a search with n or N.

If you want to keep searching for the *n*ext occurrence of the text you have specified, enter **n** after vi has found the first occurrence. If you want to search in the other direction, enter **N**. You can press the **n** key once, or a number of times. If I press **n** three times, for instance, to keep searching for **is**, the cursor will first jump to the **is** in **relish**, then to the **is** in **this**, and finally, to the word **is**, as shown in Figure 9.5.

```
                    Vegetables
        Once I knew a girl who just loved vegetables.  You
didn't dare leave this little bunny alone with a relish tray
or it would be instantly deflowered of its cauliflowerlets
and stripped clean of its carrot strips.
        But this girl is in the minority.  For cold
scientific proof, do this: on one side of a plate, put a
stack of marinated string beans; on the other side, put a
heap of smoked oysters.  Then observe carefully which gets
```

*Figure 9.4: Searching for **is** in the sample.text file*

```
                    Vegetables
        Once I knew a girl who just loved vegetables.  You
didn't dare leave this little bunny alone with a relish tray
or it would be instantly deflowered of its cauliflowerlets
and stripped clean of its carrot strips.
        But this girl is in the minority.  For cold
scientific proof, do this: on one side of a plate, put a
stack of marinated string beans; on the other side, put a
heap of smoked oysters.  Then observe carefully which gets
```

Figure 9.5: Continuing a search

If I then wanted to go back to one of the occurrences earlier in the file, I could enter **N** and the cursor would jump back to the previous occurrences of **is** marked with dotted lines in Figure 9.4. If I started at the bottom of the file and searched up through it with the **?** command, I could keep searching up with **n** and search downward with **N**.

Searches like this will continue until they reach the beginning or end of the file, then "wrap" to the other end of the file and keep going. For instance, if I keep searching upward for **is** with **N**, I will soon reach the beginning of the file. Then vi will go back to the end of the file and start searching upward from there until it reaches an occurrence of **is**.

Use special characters or exclude text to limit a search.

If you are searching for a specific word or phrase in the text and your search stops on too many other words or phrases that contain it, limit your search. You can enter more of the word or phrase you are looking for, or you can use special characters to exclude certain combinations from the search.

For instance, I want to see only the occurrences of the word **is** in my sample.text file. The special characters \< mean "at the beginning of a word," and \> mean "at the end of a word," so I could enter

   \<**is**\>

to mean "look for the word **is** and nothing else." I could also use the search pattern **[^a]** to exclude a character from the search, where **a** is a character I want to exclude. Since **is** is often combined with a **th** beginning or an **h** ending, I could (somewhat clumsily) exclude an **h** from either side of **is** this way:

   [^h]is[^h]

This would find only occurrences of **is** which did not begin or end with **h**, so it would find it as a single word. It would also, however, find **disk** or **aisle** if those words were in my file. Sometimes, however, you may find it easier to search for things by exclusion this way. For instance, if I wanted to search for **dishcloth** but not **dishes** or **radish**, I might enter

   \<**dish[^e]**

The \< would exclude any occurrence of **dish** that came in the middle of a word (**radish**); the **[^e]** would exclude **dish** with an **e** after it (**dishes**). As you practice your searches, you will find yourself becoming very expert at using these special search commands to save yourself time.

Using Colon Commands

You can use the colon and a wide variety of commands in escape mode, and return to the file at the same place you left it when you entered the colon. The following procedures show what you can do with some of the most commonly used colon commands, including setting parameters, saving your work, moving and copying text, and writing text to other files.

Set parameters for vi with :set parameter.

There are a number of different parameters you can set that affect how vi behaves. You have already seen the **:set wm = 20** command; you set it as your default in your .exrc file. But you can change the setting by a colon command. To see all of the parameters you can set, enter **:set all**. vi displays the parameters and current settings at the bottom of your screen. On my screen they look like Figure 9.6.

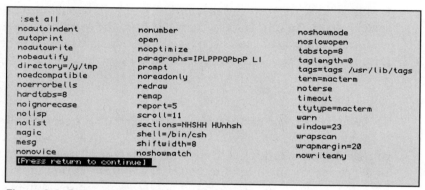

```
:set all
noautoindent          nonumber                      noshowmode
autoprint             open                          noslowopen
noautowrite           nooptimize                    tabstop=8
nobeautify            paragraphs=IPLPPPQPbpP LI      taglength=0
directory=/y/tmp      prompt                        tags=tags /usr/lib/tags
noedcompatible        noreadonly                    term=macterm
noerrorbells          redraw                        noterse
hardtabs=8            remap                         timeout
noignorecase          report=5                      ttytype=macterm
nolisp                scroll=11                     warn
nolist                sections=NHSHH HUnhsh         window=23
magic                 shell=/bin/csh                wrapscan
mesg                  shiftwidth=8                  wrapmargin=20
nonovice              noshowmatch                   nowriteany
[Press return to continue]
```

Figure 9.6: Parameters you can set with :set

You may not have all of those parameters available to you, and some of the settings will probably be different. You don't ever have to worry about most of the settings, but there are a few you should know. Use **set wm = 20** (or the longer version, **:set wrapmargin = 20**) to set the right margin of your text at 20 spaces. Use **:set number** or **:set nu** to display the number of each line in your file in the left margin, as shown in Figure 9.7.

If you look at the parameters by entering **:set all** now, you see that the **nonumber** setting has changed to **number**.

One other setting that is useful is the **autoindent**. It is set to **noauto-indent** by default. If you want to do some outlining, you can enter **:set autoindent** or **:set ai** for short. Then, if you indent lines to structure your outline, the indents will stay in effect until you go into escape mode. You can set your wrap margin to one or two, so your outline can run farther to the right on the screen, like this:

I. The main topic of an outline starts here.
   A. The subtopics are indented like this.
   B. With autoindent, it's automatic!

```
 1                        Vegetables
 2         Once I knew a girl who just loved vegetables.  You
 3   didn't dare leave this little bunny alone with a relish tray
 4   or it would be instantly deflowered of its cauliflowerlets
 5   and stripped clean of its carrot strips.
 6         But this girl is in the minority.  For cold
 7   scientific proof, do this: on one side of a plate, put a
 8   stack of marinated string beans; on the other side, put a
 9   heap of smoked oysters.  Then observe carefully which gets
10   left.  You needn't even be that fancy.  A can of salted
11   peanuts will win over the string beans, hands down, every
12   time.
13         Facts must be faced.  Vegetables simply don't taste
14   as good as most other things do.  And there isn't a single
15   vegetable, hot or cold, that stands on its own two feet the
16   way a ripe peach does, or a strawberry.  Even sweet corn
17   needs butter and salt.  It is interesting to note that
18   vegetables beginning with A are the most self-sufficient:
19   artichokes, asparagus, and avocados, which have really
20   slithered out of the fruit kingdom by this time into the
21   vegetable kingdom, no matter what the botanists say.  But
22   the farther down the alphabet you go, through rutabagas,
23   spinach, and turnips, the more hopeless they become, given
24   all the butter and salt you've got.
```

Figure 9.7: Line numbers in a vi file

To learn more about setting parameters, see *An Introduction to Display Editing with vi,* by William Joy and Mark Horton, University of California at Berkeley, 1986.

Save your work on a file.

Use **w:** while you are working on a file. It writes all your latest changes to the hard disk, and lets you go right on working; the cursor returns to its previous location.

Quit vi without saving your changes to a file.

Use **:q!** when you have made some destructive mistakes while editing or writing a file, and you want to go back to the version of the file you had before you started working on it. (Keep in mind that you'll lose any positive changes you've made, too.)

Move to a specific line of text.

If you have set the numbers parameter as described in the first step of this procedure, you can move the cursor to any line of the text by entering **:n** where **n** is a line number. For example, if I want to move the cursor to the line that begins with the word *artichokes,* I can enter **:19** and the cursor will appear under the **a** of that word. This command is an alternative to the **nG** command.

Move lines in a file using the :x,y m z command.

The **x, y,** and **z** stand for line numbers. This command *m*oves the lines between line numbers **x** and **y** to a position immediately following line number **z,** and it pushes all of the text following line **z** down to make room. For example, if I want to move the first two paragraphs of my sample.text file down below the last paragraph shown in Figure 9.6, I can enter **:2,12 m 24.** The 2 paragraphs move down and the third one moves up to the top of the file to fill the gap.

Copy lines in a file by using the :x,y co z command.

This command makes a copy of the lines from line numbers **x** to **y** and places the copy on the lines following line number **z.** It pushes all of the following text down to make room. For example, if I want to copy the first two paragraphs shown in Figure 9.6 to the place after the third paragraph, I can enter **:2,12 co 24.** The copy of the first two paragraphs appears after the third one. The original two paragraphs are still there when I scroll up to see them.

Delete lines from a file by using the :x,y d command.

This command removes the lines of text from line numbers **x** to **y.** For example, if I want to delete the first two paragraphs of my sample.text file, I can enter **:2,12 d.** The two paragraphs disappear. I can undo any of the changes in the last three steps by entering **u** after giving the colon command (before doing any other editing).

Write lines to a new file with :x,y w filename.

Use this command if you want to copy some lines from your current file into a new file. For example, if I think the first two paragraphs of my sample.text file are so important they deserve to be in a file of their own, I can enter **:2,12 w bunny.text**. A copy of the lines is made into the new file. The original lines remain unchanged.

Append lines to an existing file by using the :x,y w >> filename command.

Use this command to add some lines from one file to the end of another one. For example, if I want to add the first two lines of the third paragraph of my sample.text file to my bunny.text file, I can enter **:2,12 w >> bunny.text**. A copy of the two lines is added to the file, while the original lines remain in place.

Edit another file while in vi.

If you are working on one file and want to edit or copy something from another one, first enter **:w** to save your latest changes to the current file, then enter **:e *filename***, where *filename* is the name of the other file you want to *edit*. For example, if I want to check out the file I have just created and added to, I can enter **:e bunny.text**.

When I am done editing **bunny.text**, I can enter **:e #**. The **:e** command followed by a pound sign returns you to the previous file you were editing in the current vi session. The **:e** command is especially useful if you set a bunch of special parameters and want these settings to apply to your work in several files. If you were to exit from a file and start vi over to open another one, all the parameter settings would return to their defaults.

Replace repeated text throughout a file.

This is referred to as a global search and replace. Enter

:%s /oldtext/newtext/g

The *g* stands for global, meaning throughout the file. The *s* stands for "substitute." *oldtext* is the text you are going to replace, and *newtext* is the text you want to appear instead.

For example, if I want to replace the word *vegetable* with the word *veggie* in my sample.text file, I can do it in the following way. I have to account for the fact that some of the time the word is capitalized, and the easiest way to do this is to replace all letters except the first one. I can make the change with this command:

:%s/egetable/eggie/g

This command changes *Vegetable* to *Veggie* and *vegetables* to *veggies* as well as changing *vegetable* to *veggie*. But you have to be careful with global substitutions. You often change things in ways you don't intend. If you are changing a short word it is more wise to search for the word you want to replace, then use a replace command each time you get to it, repeating the command with a dot.

Command Summary

COMMAND	DESCRIPTION
Opening a file	
vi + filename	Opens *filename* at end
vi + / *text filename*	Opens *filename* at line where *text* occurs
vi + *n filename*	Opens *filename* at line number *n*
Moving around a file	
b	Moves cursor back one word
Ctrl-B	Scrolls back a full screen
Ctrl-D	Scrolls down half a screenful
Ctrl-E	Scrolls screen up a line
Ctrl-F	Scrolls forward a full screen
Ctrl-R or Ctrl-L	Refreshes the screen; clears stray characters
Ctrl-U	Scrolls up half a screenful
Ctrl-Y	Scrolls screen down a line
e	Moves cursor to end of current word
h	Moves cursor to the left one space
H	Moves cursor to top of screen (High)

COMMAND	DESCRIPTION
j	Moves cursor down one line
k	Moves cursor up one line
l	Moves cursor one space to the right
L	Moves cursor to bottom of screen (Low)
M	Moves cursor to middle of screen (Middle)
nG	Moves cursor to line number n
w	Moves cursor forward one word
0 (zero)	Moves cursor to beginning of line
$	Moves cursor to end of line
''	Moves cursor to previous location

Inputting Text

a	Appends text one character to right of cursor
A	Appends text at end of line
cc	Lets you change a line and continue in insert mode
cw	Lets you change a word and continue in insert mode
c)	Lets you change the rest of a sentence
c}	Lets you change the rest of a paragraph
i	Inserts text at cursor position
I	Inserts text at beginning of line
o	Opens a line to insert text below the cursor
O	Opens a line to insert text above the cursor
r	Lets you replace a character and return to escape mode

COMMAND	DESCRIPTION
Editing Text	
add	Deletes a line into buffer a
"ap	Puts yanked or deleted lines from buffer a after cursor
"aP	Puts yanked or deleted lines from buffer a before cursor
ayy	Yanks a line into buffer a
dd	Deletes a whole line
D	Deletes the rest of current line
dw	Deletes a word
J	Joins two short lines into one long one
ma	Marks a for yanking or deleting
p	Puts yanked or deleted text after cursor
P	Puts yanked or deleted text before cursor
u	Undoes last text-altering command
U	Undoes all the last changes to current line
x	Deletes a character
yw	Yanks a word (copy into buffer)
yy	Yanks a line
. (period)	Repeats previous command
"1p	Retrieves previous deletion
Searching for Text	
/*text*	Searches forward through file for *text*
?*text*	Searches backward through file for *text*
n	Continues search in same direction
N	Searches in opposite direction

COMMAND	DESCRIPTION
Setting vi Parameters	
:set ai	Sets autoindent (repeats indents you tab in for outlines)
:set all	Lists all parameters you can set
:set nu	Sets numbers (displays line numbers)
:set noic	Sets no ignore case (makes searches case-sensitive)
:set wm $= n$	Sets wrapmargin to n (sets right margin)
Saving, Moving, and Deleting Text with Colon Commands	
:e *filename*	Edit *filename*
:e #	Edit previous file
:*n*	Move cursor to line number n
:*x, y* m *z*	Move lines x through y to z
:*x,y* co *z*	Copy lines x through y to z
:*x,y* d	Delete lines x through y
:*x,y* w *filename*	Write lines x through y to *filename*
:*x,y* w $>>$ *filename*	Append lines x through y to *filename*
:%s/*oldtext*/*newtext*/g	Search for *oldtext* and replace each occurence with *newtext*
:q!	Quit vi and cancel all changes to file
:w	Save your last changes; write file to hard disk

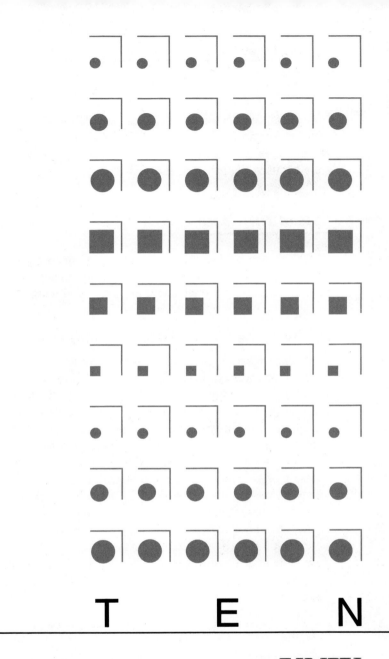

T E N

UNIX
Enhancements

This chapter describes a number of procedures for increasing your power and efficiency as a UNIX user. It tells how to customize the environment in which you work, and how to solve problems that may occur while using UNIX day-to-day.

Customizing Your Environment

This section describes how to set up your .profile and .exrc files so you can begin work on the UNIX system quickly and easily, avoiding adjustments and parameter settings at the beginning of each session.

Specifying Settings in Your .profile File

The following procedure tells how to customize the .profile file that UNIX reads every time you log in. You can add lines to this file that will set your terminal type automatically, set the paths that UNIX searches for a program when you enter a command, set aliases for pathnames you use often, and tell you who is on the system. Some of the settings are made in the form of commands, which are executed each time you log in; the calendar command you added to your .profile file in Chapter 2 is an example of such a command. Other settings are made with environment variables, which are made up of information such as the locations of important files, the values for certain variables such as time and local language, and the specification of equipment, such as your terminal type.

If you use the C-shell (your system prompt is a **%**), you have a .login file instead of a .profile file. See your UNIX User's Reference and System Administrator's Guide for information on customizing a .login file.

1. Open your .profile file.

To get into your .profile file and change things in it, move to your home directory with the **cd** command, and then use the **vi .profile** command to open the .profile file with vi.

The text of the .profile file appears. Yours may be very simple, if you haven't added anything to it except the calendar command you put there in order to run the calendar program. There will probably be a PATH line that sets the search path UNIX uses to find programs and utilities you enter commands for, and there may be some lines at the top of the file that are commented out. For example, a .profile file on our system that hasn't been modified, except by the addition of the calendar command, looks like Figure 10.1.

```
#
# User $HOME/.profile - commands executed at login time
#

PATH=/bin:/usr/bin:$HOME/bin:.         # set command search path
MAIL=/usr/spool/mail/`logname`         # mailbox location
umask 022                              # set file creation mask
export PATH MAIL
calendar
```

Figure 10.1: *A sample .profile file*

Your .profile file may not look at all like this. You may or may not have the **MAIL** path set, and you may or may not have a umask setting (the setting that puts default permissions on files you create). You may have settings not shown in the sample file.

2. Set your wrapmargin before editing your .profile file.

Each line in the .profile file has to contain everything for the setting you are making. If the text wraps to the next line, it is lost. To avoid this, enter

set wm = 0

to set your wrapmargin to 0. A long line of text may wrap to the next line on the screen now, one letter at a time, but UNIX will still see it as one long line.

3. If you always use the same type of terminal, set the TERM variable.

If you only use one terminal on the system, or if all the terminals on the system are of the same type, you can put a line in your .profile file that will set your **TERM** environment variable automatically, so you don't have to tell UNIX what kind of terminal you are using every time you log in. Use the format

TERM = *terminaltype*

and enter it below any other environment variable lines, such as the **PATH** one. My terminal is a Wyse 60, and the abbreviation for that terminal type is wy60. I would enter the following line:

TERM = wy60

If I were working with the .profile file shown in Figure 10.1, I would put this line after the **MAIL** line and before the **umask** line.

Whenever you set an environment variable in your .profile file, you must include it in the **export** line. For example, in the .profile file in Figure 10.1, I would have to add **TERM** to the **PATH** and **MAIL** variables listed after the export command.

You can also add a comment on the same line as the variable you have set, so you'll remember what it means. For example, I could enter the comment **# set terminal type** on the **TERM** line. If I did all of this to the sample .profile file shown in Figure 10.1, it would look like Figure 10.2.

```
#
# User $HOME/.profile - commands executed at login time
#

PATH=/bin:/usr/bin:$HOME/bin:.        # set command search path
MAIL=/usr/spool/mail/`logname`        # mailbox location
TERM=wy60                             # set terminal type
umask 022                             # set file creation mask
export PATH MAIL TERM
calendar
```

Figure 10.2: The .profile file with the TERM variable added

As long as I log in on Wyse 60 terminals, this .profile file will set my **TERM** environment variable correctly, so all the commands I enter from the keyboard will work in vi and in other applications. If I have to log in on a different terminal type, I will need to reset the **TERM** variable immediately after logging in, by entering

TERM = *terminaltype*

where *terminaltype* is the new terminal's type.

4. If you log in on two or more terminal types, use a tset *command in your .profile file.*

You may log in on a different terminal from your normal one now and then. It is quite common for users to have to log in on the console, the terminal directly associated with the computer, which is often set up as an ansi terminal type. If this is the case, you should put a line in your .profile file to handle the possibility of you logging in on either kind of terminal. There may also be occasions where you log in from a completely different terminal type, over a modem from another site or from a different department in a large company. You can enter a replacement for the **TERM** line in your .profile file that covers all of these possibilities. Use the **tset** command, in the following format:

eval 'tset -m *termtypex:termtypex* -m :\\?*termtypey* -r -s -Q'

Where *termtypex* is the terminal you use most often and *termtypey* is the one you use less often. The first **-m** option sends *termtypex* to the **TERM** variable if you have logged in on that type of terminal. You won't see a prompt for your terminal type, but a message stating the terminal type will be displayed at the end of the login process. If you log in on any other type of terminal, a prompt appears, like this:

TERM = (*termtypey*)

If you press the Return key, *termtypey* will be the type you have logged in on.

For example, if I normally use a Wyse 60 terminal, but sometimes log in on the ansi console, I could enter the following line:

eval 'tset -m wy60:wy60 -m :\\?ansi -r -s -Q'

This line specifies that if I log in on a Wyse 60, my terminal type is set to wy60 and I don't have to see a terminal prompt when I log in. If I log in on any other terminal type, the following prompt appears:

TERM = (ansi)

All I have to do is press the Return key if I have logged in on an ansi console, and it will be set correctly. On the rare occasions when I log in on a third type of terminal, I can enter the name for it at the TERM = (ansi) prompt.

This terminal setting line will work if your system is configured so *termtypex* connections are recognized (listed in the /etc/ttytype file), and both *termtypex* and *termtypey* are acceptable **TERM** settings. See your system administrator for more information on these prerequisites.

If you enter an **eval 'tset'** line to automate your terminal type setting, make sure you delete the TERM line in your .profile file if there is one. Take the TERM out of your export line, too. Since **eval 'tset'** is a command, you don't have to export a variable after using it. If I added my **tset** line to the sample .profile file, it would wind up looking like Figure 10.3.

```
#
# User $HOME/.profile - commands executed at login time
#

PATH=/bin:/usr/bin:$HOME/bin:.              # set command search path
MAIL=/usr/spool/mail/`logname`              # mailbox location
eval`tset -m wy60:wy60 -m:\?ansi -r -s -Q`  # set terminal type
umask 022                                   # set file creation mask
export PATH MAIL
calendar
```

Figure 10.3: *The .profile file with a tset command added*

Notice that the comment for this line has gotten pushed over a bit. That's all right, as long as you keep the pound sign in front of the comment. You can even move the comment to the previous line if you need to.

5. If you access a directory often, create an alias for it in your .profile file.

If you often have to work on files in a directory that has a long pathname, you may get tired of entering all those characters. You can make a short *alias* for the pathname, and enter it in your .profile file just like an environment variable. The format for an alias is

alias = *pathname*

where *pathname* is either the absolute pathname to a directory, or the relative pathname from your home directory, preceded by a period.

For example, if I have to update sales information in a database that is in the /x/data/fox/sales/current directory, I can create the following line in my .profile file:

sa = /x/data/fox/sales/current

If you use an alias like this, add it to the list of variables in the **export** line. If I added such an alias and a comment about it to the sample .profile file, it would look like Figure 10.4.

```
#
# User $HOME/.profile - commands executed at login time
#
PATH=/bin:/usr/bin:$HOME/bin:.          # set command search path
MAIL=/usr/spool/mail/`logname`          # mailbox location
eval `tset -m wy60:wy60 -m:\?ansi -r -s -Q`  # set terminal type
umask 022                               # set file creation mask
sa= /x/data/fox/sales/current           # alias for sales db
export PATH MAIL sa
calendar
```

Figure 10.4: *The .profile file with an alias added*

After entering such an alias in your .profile file, you can use the **cd** command with the alias, in the format **cd $alias**, to change directly to the directory from anywhere in the file system. For example, if I had put the alias shown in Figure 10.4 in my .profile file, and I wanted to get to the sales database files from somewhere deep in my home directory tree, I could enter **cd $sa** and press Return. UNIX would put me immediately into the /x/data/fox/sales/current directory.

6. If you want to use programs in a new bin directory, add its path to your command search path.

Not all commands available on your UNIX system are found in the /bin and /usr/bin directory. If you have experience with shell scripts (short programs you can execute from the Bourne or Korn shell) you may want to use commands that call on scripts in a bin directory in your home directory. Notice that in the sample .profile, there is already a $HOME/bin path specified at the end of the command search path. If you have another bin directory, and want to use scripts or programs in it in addition to the programs that are in /bin and /usr/bin, you will want to add its path to the end of your command search path.

On some systems using SCO UNIX, there is another bin directory with lots of good programs in it: the /usr/sco/bin directory. If I add this path to the search path line in the sample .profile file, I have to shorten the comment a bit, so the file now looks like Figure 10.5.

```
#
# User $HOME/.profile - commands executed at login time
#

PATH=/bin:/usr/bin:$HOME/bin:/usr/sco/bin:.  # set cmd search path
MAIL=/usr/spool/mail/`logname`               # mailbox location
eval`tset -m wy60:wy60 -m:\?ansi -r -s -Q`   # set terminal type
umask 022                                     # set file creation mask
sa=/x/data/fox/sales/current                  # alias for sales db
export PATH MAIL sa
calendar
```

Figure 10.5: *The .profile file with a new bin directory added to the command search path*

When you add a path to the command search path, make sure there are colons before and after it, but no extra spaces. Also make sure that there is a period after the last colon in the path; that ensures that you can enter a command when you are in the directory that contains the program, and the program will run.

With /usr/sco/bin added to my command search path, I can use a whole bunch of nifty commands that would be unavailable to me otherwise. Whole new worlds of power open to you when you add a new bin directory to your command search path, especially if the directory has programs written for your specific needs.

A word of caution about adding to your command search path: the order of the paths is very important. For example, with the order of paths as they are in Figure 10.5, if I enter a command that calls two different programs with the same name, one in my $HOME/bin and one in /usr/sco/bin, I will only get the program in my $HOME/bin. The command search will find a program that matches my command in my $HOME/bin, and stop searching. If I want to use the program of the same name in /usr/sco/bin, I have to change the name of the program in my $HOME/bin, or switch the order of the paths in the command search path in my .profile file, so $HOME/bin is at the end, like this:

PATH = /bin:/usr/bin:/usr/sco/bin:$HOME/bin:.

With the order in this command search path, any command I enter that calls programs of the same name in both /usr/sco/bin and $HOME/bin will use the program in /usr/sco/bin and not the one in my personal bin directory.

7. Change your system prompt.

If you want to make your system prompt more informative than a simple dollar sign, you can set the **PS1** variable to make it whatever you want. Some people think it's fun to have a long system prompt, like

This is a prompt for your next command: $ _

Others like a short prompt, since long ones take up a lot of screen space. If you work on a network that has lots of different computers, you can put an initial or two in your prompt to signify which computer you are on. I'm a traditionalist in some ways; I like to see the old dollar sign at the end of my prompt. Most people enter a space after the text of their prompt, so their commands don't get confused with the prompt. Whatever you want to enter into your prompt, enclose it in quotes, so the **PS1** line has this form:

PS1 = "*prompttext*"

For example, if I wanted to set my prompt in the sample .profile file for logging in to a computer called "Kafka," and then see the old dollar sign, I could enter the line

PS1 = "K$ "

and then add **PS1** to the **export** line. The sample .profile would look like the one in Figure 10.6.

My prompt would look like this:

K$ _

You don't have to set your prompt to look like this at all. You may want to have your user name in your prompt, if you and several other users log in on the same terminal at different times. You may have other information that you need to show at your prompt. It's completely up to you.

```
#
# User $HOME/.profile - commands executed at login time
#

PATH=/bin:/usr/bin:$HOME/bin:/usr/sco/bin:.  # set cmd search path
MAIL=/usr/spool/mail/`logname`               # mailbox location
PS1="! K$ "                                  # set prompt
eval`tset -m wy60:wy60 -m:\?ansi -r -s -Q`   # set terminal type
umask 022                                    # set file creation mask
sa=/x/data/fox/sales/current                 # alias for sales db
export PATH MAIL PS1 sa
calendar
```

Figure 10.6: *The .profile file with a system prompt setting added*

8. Add the uptime command to your .profile file.

If your system gets relatively heavy usage, you may want to find out how many users are logged in and how heavy the traffic is on the computer when you log in. To do this, just add the **uptime** command to your .profile file. If you have a calendar command at the end of the file, you can add the **uptime** command to the same line, and add a comment about both of them. If I add these things to the last line of the sample .profile file, the result is the file shown in Figure 10.7.

```
#
# User $HOME/.profile - commands executed at login time
#

PATH=/bin:/usr/bin:$HOME/bin:/usr/sco/bin:.  # set cmd search path
MAIL=/usr/spool/mail/`logname`               # mailbox location
PS1="! K$ "                                  # set prompt
eval`tset -m wy60:wy60 -m:\?ansi -r -s -Q`   # set terminal type
umask 022                                    # set file creation mask
sa=/x/data/fox/sales/current                 # alias for sales db
export PATH MAIL PS1 sa
calendar; uptime                             # show events, system use
```

Figure 10.7: *The .profile file with the* **uptime** *command added*

After adding the **uptime** command, you will see a one-line summary of how things are going on the system every time you log in. For example, I see a line like this when I log in:

09:17am up 3 days, 15:13, 4 users, load average: 3.04, 3.00, 3.00

From left to right, the entries in this line tell you the current time, the number of days, hours and minutes that your computer has been up (running), the number of users currently logged in, and finally the load average over the last minute, the last five minutes, and the last fifteen minutes.

The *load average* is the average number of processes waiting in line to run. If less than 10 have been waiting in line, the computer is working efficiently, and you can expect your tasks to be completed quickly and accurately. If you see load averages like 14.2, 12.6, 12.3, on the other hand, you can expect to have trouble carrying out calculations or printing tasks, and you may notice the cursor response slowing down even if you are just editing text with vi.

If your system often has load averages of over 10, you should recommend to your system administrator that the computer be upgraded, or another computer be added to handle the heavy usage.

Assigning vi Keystroke Shortcuts in Your .exrc File

There are many shortcuts you can set up to use in escape mode in vi. Although some of the shortcuts may be useful only in specific situations, the ones included here are some of the most widely used. You may have some of these shortcuts, or similar ones, already. If you do, you can leave them in the form you are used to, and add others to round out your vi toolkit.

Most of the following shortcuts involve assigning, or *mapping,* a command or series of commands to a keystroke or two. There are two special characters used in the mappings that follow: ^**M** and ^**[**. To create these characters, you cannot simply type ^ (a caret) and then an **M** or a **[**; the characters stand for non-printing keys, the Return key and the Escape key. To represent these keys in your .exrc file, you have to first enter **Ctrl-V**, and then press **Return** or **Escape**. The appropriate character appears. For example, if I enter **Ctrl-V** and then press **Return**, the ^M character appears.

1. Move to your home directory and open your .exrc file.

Use the **cd** command to get to your home directory, then enter **vi .exrc** to open your .exrc file. If you have created one already, it will open, showing the settings and mappings you have for vi. If you don't have a .exrc file, vi creates a new, empty one.

2. Set your wrapmargin and ignorecase parameters.

You might have entered a line to set these parameters already, as described in Chapter 9, "Advanced vi Techniques." If you haven't, enter the following line to set them.

set wm = 20 noic

The first setting, **wm = 20**, sets your wrapmargin, or right margin, at 20 spaces in from the right edge of the screen.

The second setting, **noic**, stands for *no i*gnore *c*ase, which means that the case of letters you type is distinguished by the system when you are searching for specific strings of text (for example, *A* will be seen as different from *a*).

For more information on these parameters, see the first section of Chapter 9.

3. Use map] to set wrapmargin and indent settings for outlining.

If you do lots of outlining, enter the following line in your .exrc file. This allows you to press the **]** key in escape mode in vi, and begin outlining immediately, without having to set any parameters:

map] :se wm = 1 ai^M

Make sure you enter the **^M** by first entering **Ctrl-V** and then pressing **Return**.

The settings are for a wide right margin, and for autoindent. This means you can indent once and then just press return at the end of each line and get the same indent. For more information on this setting, see the "Using Colon Commands" section in Chapter 9.

4. Abbreviate "from mark a to mark b."

If you want to do anything with blocks of text, you have to mark them. This principle was introduced in Chapter 9, but only in terms of using a single mark. If you want to do lots of yanking, deleting, and moving of text blocks, you need to mark the start and end of each block. Type **ma** (mark a) in escape mode at the beginning of the first line of the block and type **mb** (mark b) at the beginning of the last line in the block.

Once you have marked a text block in this way, you can abbreviate the phrase "from mark a to mark b" and then map appropriate keystrokes to the functions that act on the marked text block. Enter the following line in your .exrc file to abbreviate the text block marking phrase:

ab aa 'a,'b

This line, a classic in brevity, says to abbreviate the phrase **'a,'b** (from mark a to mark b) with the letters **aa**. So whenever you see the letters **aa** in the mappings that follow, you can interpret them to mean "from mark a to mark b."

5. Use **map ;y** *to yank marked lines to buffer a.*

This line will make it easy for you to yank a block of text at one time and put it back into the file later. This is very convenient if you have a block of text that you know will be repeated, but you don't know where yet. If you just yanked the block without putting it into buffer a, it would be lost the minute you did any other editing.

Enter the following line in your .exrc file to make it easy to yank a block of text into buffer a.

map ;y :aa ya a^M

Enter the **^M** by typing **Ctrl-V** and pressing **Return**.

The line specifies that the keystrokes **;y** will yank the block of text between mark a and mark b and save it in buffer a. Use these keystrokes whenever you want to yank a block of text and save it for later use. Just make sure you don't use it when there is already something you want to save in buffer a. New text that you yank into buffer a overwrites any text that is already there.

6. Use **map ;d** *to delete marked lines to buffer a.*

If you want to delete some text and save it to put back into the file later, you can mark the block with a and b, then use the **;d** to delete the text block and save it in buffer a.

Enter the following line in your .exrc file to make it easy to delete a block of text into buffer a.

map ;d :aa d a^M

Remember to enter the **^M** by typing **Ctrl-V** and pressing **Return**.

The line says that the keystroke combination **;d** will delete the block of text between mark a and mark b and put it in buffer a. The only thing you have to be careful about when you use this mapping is that you might overwrite something that is already in buffer a.

7. Use map ;p to put the contents of buffer a at the cursor location.

Use this command to put a block of text you have saved in buffer a back into the file at the cursor location. Enter the following line in your .exrc file to enable this "shortput" command.

map ;p "ap ^M

Enter the **^M** by typing **Ctrl-V** and pressing **Return**.

The line says that **;p** will put the contents of buffer a after the cursor. Notice that buffer a is specified in the line, so you can't use this command to put the contents of other named buffers (b, c and so on) with this shortcut. You have to use the full commands (for instance, **"bp** puts the contents of buffer b at the cursor location).

8. Use map ;m to move marked lines to the cursor location.

You learned how to move a few lines of text at a time with the **d** and **p** commands in Chapter 9. If you use marks and the **;m** command, you can move as big a block of text as you want, and do it with just one command. Enter the following line in your .exrc file to enable moving of blocks of text with the **;m** command.

map ;m :aa m .^M

Enter the **^M** by typing **Ctrl-V** and pressing **Return**.

The line specifies that the keystroke combination **;m** will move the block of text between mark a and mark b to the current cursor location.

The period, which often stands for the current directory in UNIX commands, stands for current cursor location here. This command does not make use of a named buffer (such as buffer a) so you have to move the block of text before placing an a or b mark anyplace else.

9. *Uppercase a word with* map ;c

This shortcut is great if you have to change some words from lowercase to uppercase letters. Enter the following line in your .exrc file:

map ;c dWi^M^[O^p:s/.*/\u&/^MkJJ

Enter each **^M** by typing **Ctrl-V** and pressing **Return;** enter the **^[** by typing **Ctrl-V** and pressing **Escape.**

You can use the shortcut for a certain number of words if you enter the number before the semi-colon. For example, to uppercase two words, you would enter

    2;c

This version of the command will not work on groups of words that are on more than one line, however.

10. *Add comments to your mapping lines.*

To add a comment in your .exrc file, you must start a new line with double quotation marks, and then enter a comment that is less than a line long. For example, if you entered short comments for the lines described in this section, your .exrc file would look like Figure 10.8.

```
"Sample .exrc file
"Set these options:
set wm=20 noic
"Set options for outlining:
map ] :se wm=0 ai^M
"Abbreviate 'a,'b with aa:
ab aa 'a,'b
"Yank (copy) lines marked a to b to buffer a:
map ;y :aa ya a^M
"Delete lines marked a to b to buffer a:
map ;d :aa d a^M
"Put contents of buffer a here:
map ;p "ap^M
"Move lines marked a to b to here:
map ;m :aa m .^M
"Put words in uppercase letters:
map ;c dWi^M^[O^p:s/.*/\u&/^MkJJ
```

Figure 10.8: A commented .exrc file

Changing Your Password

If you need to enter a new password when you first log in, or if you need to change your password to protect the privacy of the system, enter the command

passwd

at the system prompt. UNIX prompts you for your old password, and then prompts you for a new one, as explained in detail in Chapter 1.

If you ever forget your password, see your system administrator, who can force the system to accept a new one for you.

Using Shell Escapes

There are many times when you want to get out of something you are doing in UNIX and take a look at something else. The most common example is when you need something in a different file than the one you are working on, and you can't remember for sure if the file is in your working directory. UNIX provides shell escapes for this situation. You can put your work in a program on hold temporarily and give one or more commands to UNIX from outside the program, then return to it. While you are outside the program, you are giving commands to a shell, a different shell than the one you were using for the program. To refer to the Unix cafe again, you have ordered your main course from your regular waiter, but you call another waiter to bring you some water. (For a more thorough explanation of this concept, reread the first section of Chapter 1.)

The following procedures explain how to use shell escapes to get out of various programs, and how to return from the shell escape in each case.

Shell Escapes from vi

There are two ways to escape to a shell from vi. One, using the exclamation point, is a quick escape, limited to one command; the other is for more extended work from the system prompt. Both escapes require that you be in escape mode, naturally.

1. Get into escape mode from insert mode.

If you are in insert mode, press the Escape key.

2. To escape for a single command, enter :!commandname.

If you want to do only one thing outside vi, and then come right back to where you were, use the colon command :!*commandname*, where *commandname* is a system command. For example, you can list the files in your working directory with the command :!**lf**.

If you have not saved your work since modifying the vi file, a message appears:

No write since last change

Then the file listing is displayed, and another message appears:

Press return to continue

Press Return, and you return to your vi file just where you left it.

3. Use :sh to escape to the shell.

If you want to do several things outside of vi before you come back to it, you can bring up a system prompt with the :**sh** command. You can enter as many commands as you want at the prompt. For example, you can enter **lf** to list the files in the working directory, and then use **more** to read one of the files and get information you need in your vi file.

You can also change directories in the shell, and vi other files. None of the things you do from the escape shell affect the situation in your login shell, the one you left behind when you left vi. Just don't reopen the file you were working on in vi. Any changes you make from the escape shell to that file will be overwritten when you go back in and save it.

4. Use the exit command to return from the shell to vi.

When you have finished your work at the system prompt, enter exit and the shell prompt disappears. You return to your vi file where you left it.

It is easy to forget which shell you are in if you escape and do a number of things from the system prompt, or if you escape from vi, then escape again from the new shell.

If you forget to return to your vi file, and try to log out from a shell you have escaped to, you will get an error message that says you are not in the login shell. Just enter **exit** and you will return to your vi file. Then you can save and quit the vi file and log out of your login shell.

Shell Escapes from E-mail

You can also escape from e-mail, whether you are reading messages or creating a message.

1. Use !commandname
to escape while reading messages.

If you are looking at the message list and the cursor is at the ampersand mail prompt, enter **!commandname**, where *commandname* is a system command. If you are reading a message, read to the end of it or press the Delete key to get out of it, and then enter **!commandname** to escape from mail. You can give any system command you like for *commandname*. For example, if I want to see a list of the mailbox files that I can save a message to, I can enter

   !lf /u/tomc/News

The results of the command are displayed, the system prompt and an exclamation mark appear, and then you are given the ampersand mail cursor again. If your message list has scrolled off the top of your screen, just use the **h** command to display it again.

2. Use ˜ !commandname
to escape to a shell if you are creating a message.

You can escape to a shell while writing a message by typing ˜**!commandname**, where *commandname* is a system command. For example, if you want to know the name of a file you're thinking of including in a message, enter ˜ **!lf**.

The results of your command are displayed, the system prompt and an exclamation mark appear. You are sent back to the mail program, and a **(continue)** message appears, indicating that you can go on creating your message.

Shell Escapes from Other Programs

Although the exclamation point is commonly used to escape to a shell from most UNIX programs, the mode from which you can escape is different for each program. In Office Portfolio, SCO Professional, and other menu interface programs, you can usually escape by typing !*commandname* if a menu is active. After the results of your command are displayed, you usually see a message asking you to press any key to continue; pressing a key returns you to the menu you left. In database programs, you can usually escape from the command line and return to the command line after seeing the results of your command.

If you cannot figure out how to do a shell escape from a program, ask an experienced user, or see the documentation for the program.

Using On-Line Manual Pages

On many UNIX systems, you can learn about the uses and options for a command before you use it. At the system prompt, give the command

   man *commandname*

and press the Return key.

Information about the command appears, including the syntax you should use, a description of the effect of the command and its options, and the files affected by the command. There are often examples of how to use the command, which can be particularly helpful. The same information is listed alphabetically in the *UNIX User's Reference* book.

Using UNIX over a Modem

If your terminal is connected to your UNIX system by means of a modem and telephone lines, use the following procedure to prepare for using the modem. Make sure your terminal or computer is set up properly for the use of the modem, and that it is compatible with it.

1. Turn off the terminal and modem and make all necessary configuration settings.

Before you set up your modem and terminal, make sure the power switches on both are turned off. Then make sure your terminal or computer has the correct settings for communication over your type of modem. Settings such as the baud rate, handshake, parity, character size, and stop bits must be correct in order for your computer or terminal to communicate over a modem. To make sure you have these settings correct, get help with them from your system administrator. Once they are set correctly, you don't have to change them.

2. Connect the interface cable, phone line, and power cords of the terminal and the modem.

Connect the terminal to the modem by using the correct connector cable. Make sure you are connecting the cable to the right jack or plug on the modem, and the right port on the computer or terminal. Again, see your system administrator for help in getting the connection right the first time; you won't ever need help with it again. Connect the phone line from the modem to a telephone outlet. Plug in the power cords of the modem and the computer or terminal, using a power source that is protected from surges.

3. Turn on the modem and terminal.

Turn on the power of the modem first, and check the power light if there is one. Then turn on your computer or terminal. If you are using a computer, start the software program used for dialing in on a modem.

When you see the terminal cursor or the cursor of the modem software, you are ready to dial in. If your terminal or computer is not working properly, see your system administrator for help.

4. Dial in to connect to the computer.

Either use the automatic dialing utility of your computer's modem program, or dial in on your terminal's keyboard. If the telephone connection is successful, you will hear a high-pitched sound, then see either a login prompt or a prompt for a machine name. If the connection is not successful, hang up and try again; it often takes two or three attempts.

5. Name and log in to a computer
if it is on a network, then log in to your account.

If your UNIX system consists of a network of computers, you have to choose a machine (computer) to log in to, and give that machine's password. When you have done this successfully, the login prompt for the machine appears.

If you have only one computer on your UNIX system, the login prompt appears when you make the telephone connection.

When you see your login prompt, you are ready to log in, as described in Chapter 1, "Getting Started."

Solving Major Problems

This section covers two serious problems that can stop your work on your UNIX system. If your terminal does not respond to anything you do, you have either a hung terminal or a hung process on the computer. *Hung* means that the terminal or process is still operational, but that for some reason it is "hung up" on something. The whole computer may be hung or down, but this happens less frequently, so you should eliminate the less extreme possibilities before you contact your system administrator and ask for help. Often something is hung up because of a simple error you have made.

Restarting a Hung Terminal

This procedure will correct problems that are caused by something you did to your terminal, or something that happened to your terminal that has nothing to do with the rest of the system. Unless you are sure you know what caused the problems, try the steps of the procedure in order; the first steps eliminate many common causes of the problem.

1. Try to escape from the program you are using.

Programs can die or go to sleep on you. Try the following keystrokes to see if any of them can let you escape from the program to the system prompt.

Return	Escape
Delete	Break
Ctrl-x	Ctrl-\
q	

Try each key or keystroke combination several times, just to make sure.

2. Try to reset your terminal, then turn it off and on.

Enter the command **tset** and press the Return key, even if no characters appear on the screen when you type. If this has no effect, try **Ctrl-J tset Ctrl-J**. Then turn off your terminal, turn it back on, and press the Return key when the cursor comes into view. If the terminal seems to be working, enter the command **tset** again. Then enter the command **stty sane** to set things in a "sane" state for your terminal. If you have special settings for your terminal that are controlled by your .profile file, enter . **.profile** while in your home directory to get your special settings back.

3. Check your terminal's internal settings.

You may have accidentally entered a keystroke combination that locks up or disables your terminal. Use your terminal's internal configuration utility to check the settings. You'll need to ask a user who is familiar with the terminal to go over the settings with you, comparing yours to those of a terminal that is working, to see if any settings on your terminal are wrong.

4. Try to log out.

Do this as a last resort. Enter **Ctrl-d** or the word **exit**, even if you can't see any letters on the screen.

5. Go on to the hung process procedure below.

If steps 1 to 4 are of no help, then you can assume that there is a problem with either a process you are running on the computer, or a problem with the whole computer. If other users are complaining about the computer being down, that will be the problem. If other users are having no trouble with the computer, then you can assume you have a hung process.

Killing a Hung Process

This procedure tells you how to terminate or "kill" a process that is either stopped or running mindlessly over and over. There is no way for you to tell which is happening if your terminal is not responding, but this procedure tells how to take care of both stopped and runaway processes.

1. Log in on another terminal.

Log in just as you would on your own terminal. If your UNIX system consists of a network of different computers, make sure you log into the same computer that your hung terminal is attached to.

2. Check your processes.

When you have logged in on another terminal, enter the command **ps -fu** *loginname*, where *loginname* is your own login name. If I enter the command **ps -fu tomc**, I see this result:

UID	PID	PPID	C	STIME	TTY	TIME	COMMAND
tomc	13558	1	0	09:25:59	005	0:02	-csh
tomc	13646	13558	0	09:28:02	005	0:01	vi calendar
tomc	13899	1	0	09:25:59	002	0:02	-csh
tomc	13973	13899	8	09:28:17	002	0:00	ps -fu tomc

This is a listing of the most recent processes I have run on the computer. The key thing to look for in your listing is the *process identification number* (PID) of the last process you ran before you logged in on the second terminal. In the sample above, look at the TTY (terminal) numbers of the different processes. They change from 005 to 002; the last process I ran on TTY 005 is PID 13646. That's the hung process.

3. Terminate the hung process.

Make sure you have the correct identification number of the process you want to kill. Then enter the command **kill -15 *PID***, where *PID* is the process identification number. For example, if I was terminating PID 13646, I would enter **kill -15 13646**.

Look on the screen of your hung terminal. You may see a login prompt, or just the system prompt. Press the Return key a couple of times, just to make sure you aren't hung anymore, then log in if you need to. Log out of the second terminal, and you can go back to work on your own terminal.

If you still get no response from your terminal, you may have to enter a sledgehammer form of the kill command, **kill -9 *PID***. In some rare cases, you even have to kill the "parent" process of the hung one. In my example, that would be PID 13558 shown in the listing.

If all of these efforts fail to get any response out of your hung terminal, see your system administrator.

Command Summary

COMMAND	DESCRIPTION
man *commandname*	Explain uses and options of commandname
:!*commandname* or :sh	Shell escapes from vi
!*commandname* ~!*commandname*	Shell escapes from mail program
!*commandname*	Shell escapes from applications

COMMAND	DESCRIPTION
Return Escape Delete Break Ctrl-x Ctrl-\ q	Keystrokes to use when terminal is hung
kill -15 PID	Terminates hung process

INDEX

A

A command (vi), 37, 209
a command (vi), 37–38, 209
a in permission commands, 86
absolute path commands, 75
ac command (Office Portfolio), 146
accounts, 6
addition with SCO Professional, 174
addresses, worksheet, 168
ae command (Office Portfolio), 147
aliases for paths, 232–233
alphabetical order, sorting database
    records by, 193
Alt-H key with Microsoft Word, 161
ampersands (&) with message lists, 52
ansi terminals, 97
apostrophes (') with vi, 207
APPEND command
    (FoxBASE+), 194
appending text with vi, 209, 221
Application command (Office
    Portfolio), 131, 137
applications
    with Office Portfolio, 137–138
    printing from, 124–125
archives
    adding files to, 102–105
    extracting files from, 105–108
    saving files to, 96–102
    tape, 108–110
arguments with commands, 14, 16

B

arrow keys
    with Microsoft Word, 161
    with Office Portfolio, 149
asterisks (*)
    with SCO Professional, 174
    for wildcards, 82
autoindent setting (vi), 218–219

b command (vi), 27, 205
backing up files
    command summary for, 110–111
    directory for, 93–95
    and extracting, 105–108
    onto floppy disks, 96–105
    problems with, 109–110
    on tape, 108–110
    for worksheets, 179–180, 183
Backspace key
    location of, 8–9
    with Office Portfolio, 143
    problems with, 19
binary (bin) files
    directories for, 74–75
    path for, 233–235
blind carbon copies, 62
blocking factor, 100–101
blocks, .exrc file settings for, 238–239
Bourne shell, 3, 13

for SCO Professional, 178
INSERT BEFORE command
 (FoxBASE+), 194
inserting text with vi, 25, 209

J

J command (vi), 214
j command (vi), 28, 30
joining lines with vi, 214
justification of worksheet labels, 172

K

k command (vi), 28, 30, 206
kernel, 3–5
keyboard, 2, 8–9
killing hung processes, 249–250

L

l command, 85
l command (mail), 61–62
L command (vi), 207
l command (vi), 27, 206
label form command (FoxBASE+), 197
labeling floppy disks, 102
labels
  mailing, printing, 197
  on worksheets, 172–173
legends for SCO Professional graphs, 176
less than sign (<) in vi searches, 217
lf command, 41, 70–73, 78–79, 83–84,
  92, 203
list command (FoxBASE+), 192
listing
  database files and records, 191–192
  files, 41, 70–73, 78–79, 83–84, 92,
  101, 105, 203

users, 13–15
load average, 237
local printing, 114–115
logging in, 7–12
  to console, 96–97
  by modem, 245–247
  preparation for, 5–7
  problems in, 18–20
  startup file for, 41–42
logging out, 17–18
  of console, 102
  with hung terminals, 249
Logical type (FoxBASE+), 188
.login file, 41, 79
logout command, 42
lp command, 120–123
lpstat command, 123
ls command, 70

M

˜M command (mail), 51, 63
˜m command (mail), 58
M command (vi), 207
:m command (vi), 220
^M for vi shortcut mapping, 237
ma command (vi), 213
magnetic tape archives, 108–110
mail problem message, 51
mail program. *See also* e-mail
  (electronic mail)
  command summary for, 65–66
  deleting messages with, 54–55
  exiting, 63–64
  forwarding messages with, 61
  printing messages with, 61–62
  problems with, 64–65
  reading messages with, 51–58, 64–66
  replying to messages with, 58–61, 66
  saving messages with, 55–57
  sending messages with, 48–51, 63
mailing labels, printing, 197
.mailrc file, 78

Selections from The SYBEX Library

OPERATING SYSTEMS

The ABC's of DOS 4
Alan R. Miller
275pp. Ref. 583-2

This step-by-step introduction to using DOS 4 is written especially for beginners. Filled with simple examples, *The ABC's of DOS 4* covers the basics of hardware, software, disks, the system editor EDLIN, DOS commands, and more.

ABC's of MS-DOS (Second Edition)
Alan R. Miller
233pp. Ref. 493-3

This handy guide to MS-DOS is all many PC users need to manage their computer files, organize floppy and hard disks, use EDLIN, and keep their computers organized. Additional information is given about utilities like Sidekick, and there is a DOS command and program summary. The second edition is fully updated for Version 3.3.

DOS Assembly Language Programming
Alan R. Miller
365pp. 487-9

This book covers PC-DOS through 3.3, and gives clear explanations of how to assemble, link, and debug 8086, 8088, 80286, and 80386 programs. The example assembly language routines are valuable for students and programmers alike.

DOS Instant Reference
SYBEX Prompter Series
Greg Harvey
Kay Yarborough Nelson
220pp. Ref. 477-1, 4 3/4" × 8"

A complete fingertip reference for fast, easy on-line help:command summaries, syntax, usage and error messages. Organized by function—system commands, file commands, disk management, directories, batch files, I/O, networking, programming, and more. Through Version 3.3.

DOS User's Desktop Companion
SYBEX Ready Reference Series
Judd Robbins
969pp. Ref. 505-0

This comprehensive reference covers DOS commands, batch files, memory enhancements, printing, communications and more information on optimizing each user's DOS environment. Written with step-by-step instructions and plenty of examples, this volume covers all versions through 3.3.

Encyclopedia DOS
Judd Robbins
1030pp. Ref. 699-5

A comprehensive reference and user's guide to all versions of DOS through 4.0. Offers complete information on every DOS command, with all possible switches and parameters -- plus examples of effective usage. An invaluable tool.

Essential OS/2
(Second Edition)
Judd Robbins
445pp. Ref. 609-X

Written by an OS/2 expert, this is the guide to the powerful new resources of the OS/2 operating system standard edition 1.1 with presentation manager. Robbins introduces the standard edition, and details multitasking under OS/2, and the range of commands for installing, starting up, configuring, and running applications. For Version 1.1 Standard Edition.

Essential PC-DOS
(Second Edition)
Myril Clement Shaw
Susan Soltis Shaw
332pp. Ref. 413-5

An authoritative guide to PC-DOS, including version 3.2. Designed to make experts out of beginners, it explores everything from disk management to batch file programming. Includes an 85-page command summary. Through Version 3.2.

Graphics Programming
Under Windows
Brian Myers
Chris Doner
646pp. Ref. 448-8

Straightforward discussion, abundant examples, and a concise reference guide to graphics commands make this book a must for Windows programmers. Topics range from how Windows works to programming for business, animation, CAD, and desktop publishing. For Version 2.

Hard Disk Instant Reference
SYBEX Prompter Series
Judd Robbins
256pp. Ref. 587-5, 4 ¾" × 8"

Compact yet comprehensive, this pocket-sized reference presents the essential information on DOS commands used in managing directories and files, and in optimizing disk configuration. Includes a survey of third-party utility capabilities. Through DOS 4.0.

The IBM PC-DOS Handbook
(Third Edition)
Richard Allen King
359pp. Ref. 512-3

A guide to the inner workings of PC-DOS 3.2, for intermediate to advanced users and programmers of the IBM PC series. Topics include disk, screen and port control, batch files, networks, compatibility, and more. Through Version 3.3.

Inside DOS: A Programmer's
Guide
Michael J. Young
490pp. Ref. 710-X

A collection of practical techniques (with source code listings) designed to help you take advantage of the rich resources intrinsic to MS-DOS machines. Designed for the experienced programmer with a basic understanding of C and 8086 assembly language, and DOS fundamentals.

Mastering DOS
(Second Edition)
Judd Robbins
722pp. Ref. 555-7

"The most useful DOS book." This seven-part, in-depth tutorial addresses the needs of users at all levels. Topics range from running applications, to managing files and directories, configuring the system, batch file programming, and techniques for system developers. Through Version 4.

MS-DOS Advanced
Programming
Michael J. Young
490pp. Ref. 578-6

Practical techniques for maximizing performance in MS-DOS software by making best use of system resources. Topics include functions, interrupts, devices, multitasking, memory residency and more, with examples in C and assembler. Through Version 3.3.

MS-DOS Handbook
(Third Edition)
Richard Allen King
362pp. Ref. 492-5
This classic has been fully expanded and revised to include the latest features of MS-DOS Version 3.3. Two reference books in one, this title has separate sections for programmer and user. Multi-DOS partitons, 3 ½-inch disk format, batch file call and return feature, and comprehensive coverage of MS-DOS commands are included. Through Version 3.3.

MS-DOS Power User's Guide,
Volume I
(Second Edition)
Jonathan Kamin
482pp. Ref. 473-9
A fully revised, expanded edition of our best-selling guide to high-performance DOS techniques and utilities—with details on Version 3.3. Configuration, I/O, directory structures, hard disks, RAM disks, batch file programming, the ANSI.SYS device driver, more. Through Version 3.3.

Programmers Guide to
the OS/2 Presentation Manager
Michael J. Young
683pp. Ref. 569-7
This is the definitive tutorial guide to writing programs for the OS/2 Presentation Manager. Young starts with basic architecture, and explores every important feature including scroll bars, keyboard and mouse interface, menus and accelerators, dialogue boxes, clipboards, multitasking, and much more.

Programmer's Guide to
Windows
(Second Edition)
David Durant
Geta Carlson
Paul Yao
704pp. Ref. 496-8
The first edition of this programmer's guide was hailed as a classic. This new edition covers Windows 2 and Windows/386 in depth. Special emphasis is given to over fifty new routines to the Windows interface, and to preparation for OS/2 Presentation Manager compatibility.

Understanding DOS 3.3
Judd Robbins
678pp. Ref. 648-0
This best selling, in-depth tutorial addresses the needs of users at all levels with many examples and hands-on exercises. Robbins discusses the fundamentals of DOS, then covers manipulating files and directories, using the DOS editor, printing, communicating, and finishes with a full section on batch files.

Understanding Hard Disk
Management on the PC
Jonathan Kamin
500pp. Ref. 561-1
This title is a key productivity tool for all hard disk users who want efficient, error-free file management and organization. Includes details on the best ways to conserve hard disk space when using several memory-guzzling programs. Through DOS 4.

Up & Running
with Your Hard Disk
Klaus M Rubsam
140pp. Ref. 666-9
A far-sighted, compact introduction to hard disk installation and basic DOS use. Perfect for PC users who want the practical essentials in the shortest possible time. In 20 basic steps, learn to choose your hard disk, work with accessories, back up data, use DOS utilities to save time, and more.

Up & Running with Windows
286/386
Gabriele Wentges
132pp. Ref. 691-X
This handy 20-step overview gives PC users all the essentials of using Windows - - whether for evaluating the software, or getting a fast start. Each self-contained lesson takes just 15 minutes to one hour to complete.

SYBEX

TO JOIN THE SYBEX MAILING LIST OR ORDER BOOKS PLEASE COMPLETE THIS FORM

NAME _____ COMPANY _____

STREET _____ CITY _____

STATE _____ ZIP _____

☐ PLEASE MAIL ME MORE INFORMATION ABOUT **SYBEX** TITLES

ORDER FORM (There is no obligation to order)

PLEASE SEND ME THE FOLLOWING:

TITLE	QTY	PRICE
_____	____	____
_____	____	____
_____	____	____
_____	____	____

TOTAL BOOK ORDER ____ $____

CUSTOMER SIGNATURE _____

SHIPPING AND HANDLING PLEASE ADD $2.00 PER BOOK VIA UPS ____

FOR OVERSEAS SURFACE ADD $5.25 PER BOOK PLUS $4.40 REGISTRATION FEE ____

FOR OVERSEAS AIRMAIL ADD $18.25 PER BOOK PLUS $4.40 REGISTRATION FEE ____

CALIFORNIA RESIDENTS PLEASE ADD APPLICABLE SALES TAX ____

TOTAL AMOUNT PAYABLE ____

☐ CHECK ENCLOSED   ☐ VISA
☐ MASTERCARD   ☐ AMERICAN EXPRESS

ACCOUNT NUMBER _____

EXPIR. DATE _____ DAYTIME PHONE _____

CHECK AREA OF COMPUTER INTEREST:

☐ BUSINESS SOFTWARE

☐ TECHNICAL PROGRAMMING

☐ OTHER: _____

THE FACTOR THAT WAS MOST IMPORTANT IN YOUR SELECTION:

☐ THE SYBEX NAME

☐ QUALITY

☐ PRICE

☐ EXTRA FEATURES

☐ COMPREHENSIVENESS

☐ CLEAR WRITING

☐ OTHER _____

OTHER COMPUTER TITLES YOU WOULD LIKE TO SEE IN PRINT:

_____

_____

OCCUPATION

☐ PROGRAMMER   ☐ TEACHER

☐ SENIOR EXECUTIVE   ☐ HOMEMAKER

☐ COMPUTER CONSULTANT   ☐ RETIRED

☐ SUPERVISOR   ☐ STUDENT

☐ MIDDLE MANAGEMENT   ☐ OTHER:

☐ ENGINEER/TECHNICAL   _____

☐ CLERICAL/SERVICE

☐ BUSINESS OWNER/SELF EMPLOYED

CHECK YOUR LEVEL OF COMPUTER USE

☐ NEW TO COMPUTERS

☐ INFREQUENT COMPUTER USER

☐ FREQUENT USER OF ONE SOFTWARE
  PACKAGE:
  NAME _____

☐ FREQUENT USER OF MANY SOFTWARE
  PACKAGES

☐ PROFESSIONAL PROGRAMMER

OTHER COMMENTS:

_____
_____
_____
_____
_____
_____
_____
_____

PLEASE FOLD, SEAL, AND MAIL TO SYBEX

- -

SYBEX, INC.
2021 CHALLENGER DR. #100
ALAMEDA, CALIFORNIA USA
                              94501

SYBEX

SEAL

SYBEX Computer Books
are different.

Here is why . . .

At SYBEX, each book is designed with you in mind. Every manuscript is carefully selected and supervised by our editors, who are themselves computer experts. We publish the best authors, whose technical expertise is matched by an ability to write clearly and to communicate effectively. Programs are thoroughly tested for accuracy by our technical staff. Our computerized production department goes to great lengths to make sure that each book is well-designed.

In the pursuit of timeliness, SYBEX has achieved many publishing firsts. SYBEX was among the first to integrate personal computers used by authors and staff into the publishing process. SYBEX was the first to publish books on the CP/M operating system, microprocessor interfacing techniques, word processing, and many more topics.

Expertise in computers and dedication to the highest quality product have made SYBEX a world leader in computer book publishing. Translated into fourteen languages, SYBEX books have helped millions of people around the world to get the most from their computers. We hope we have helped you, too.

For a complete catalog of our publications:

SYBEX, Inc. 2021 Challenger Drive, #100, Alameda, CA 94501
Tel: (415) 523-8233/(800) 227-2346   Telex: 336311
Fax: (415) 523-2373

VI COMMANDS

Command	Description
x	Deletes a character.
. (dot)	Repeats previous command.
0 (zero)	Moves cursor to beginning of line.
$	Moves cursor to end of line.

OFFICE PORTFOLIO

Command	Description
op	Start Office Portfolio.
Ctrl-B	Backspace; deletes characters.
Ctrl-H	Moves cursor left one character.
Ctrl-J	Moves cursor down one line.
Ctrl-K	Moves cursor up one line.
Ctrl-L	Moves cursor right one character.
Ctrl-N	Moves cursor to next word.
Ctrl-O	Opens a new line.
Ctrl-P	Moves cursor to previous word.
Ctrl-V	Puts you in and out of Overstrike mode.
Escape key (ESC)	Escape; exits a form without accepting new data.
F1	Calls up Help.
F2	Exits form or application.
Return key (↵)	Selects option or accepts data in a field.
!	Lets you enter system prompt commands.

MICROSOFT WORD

Command	Description
word *filename*	Opens or creates specified file using Word.
↑ or Ctrl-K	Moves to line above.
↓ or Ctrl-J	Moves to line below.
← or Ctrl-G	Moves to previous character.
→ or Ctrl-L	Moves to next character.
Ctrl-PgUp or Ctrl-C-U	Moves to beginning of document.
Ctrl-PgDn or Ctrl-C-D	Moves to end of document.